The Bread Machine Cookbook II

Donna Rathmell German

Bristol Publishing Enterprises, Inc.
San Leandro, California

A Nitty Gritty® Cookbook

Printed in the United States of America.

ISBN 1-55867-037-8

Cover design: Frank Paredes
Cover Photography: John Benson
Food stylist: Stephanie Greenleigh

CONTENTS

There was an old woman who lived in a shoe.
She had so many children she didn't know what to do.
She gave them some broth and some hot, homemade bread
and kissed them all sweetly and put them to bed.

This book is dedicated to my three daughters,
Rachel, Katie and Helen, and to my husband, Lee.

I would like to thank the
Marine Sentry Guards at the U.S. Naval Academy
and the dozens of midshipmen who helped us
eat hundreds of test loaves.

HOW TO USE THIS BOOK

Each recipe in this book was developed and tested so that it may be made on any bread machine on the market.

Three different sizes of loaves are given, which enables you to chose whichever size fits your machine or whichever size is appropriate to your needs. I must caution that you may not make a loaf larger than your machine manufacturer recommends. However, you may make a smaller loaf.

Care has been taken to provide directions specific to all machines, if applicable. If no specific instructions are given, recipes were tested on the basic white cycle.

Owners of WELBILT and DAK machines should read the recipes from the bottom up. In other words, yeast should always be the first ingredient. All other machines should place the ingredients in the machine as stated in the recipe with the liquids first and the dry ingredients last. In all cases, the yeast should not touch the liquids until the cycle begins. This is especially important when using the timer.

Please read the instruction manual for your machine carefully. It will tell you exactly how to operate your specific machine.

INFORMATION ABOUT BREAD MACHINES

This chapter should help you to understand how to use your specific machine or to select which machine to buy to fit your needs. I cannot tell you which machine to buy, but I can provide you with information to assist you in making a decision. Every attempt has been made to include information on every manufacturer as well as every model. This is, however, a rapidly growing market with new machines and models constantly being introduced. Updates on this chapter may be done periodically.

If you are in the market for a bread machine, look carefully at the tables which indicate the various cycles and capacities. Select the machine which will meet your requirements.

Please remember to read the instruction manual of your machine as I do not cover all aspects of how to use your machine. Rather I provide hints for use.

The following table lists the time required to bake loaves (including cooling cycles) in the various machines on different cycles. (Hours.Minutes)

	Basic White	Dough	Rapid Rise	Crusty French	Sweet Bread	Whole Grains
DAK	4.40	2.20	n/a	4.40	5.00	n/a
Hitachi						
HB-B101	4.10	1.40	2.50	n/a	n/a	n/a
HB-B201	4.10	1.40	2.50	n/a	n/a	n/a
Maxim BB-1	3.30	1.20	2.40	3.30	n/a	2.20
National/Panasonic:						
SD-BT6N/SD-BT6P	4.15	2.20	2.45	7.00	n/a	n/a
SD-BT51N/SD-BT51P	4.00	1.55	2.45	n/a	n/a	n/a
100% Whole Wheat	4.00	2.25	3.00	n/a	n/a	5.00
Regal						
Deluxe	4.10	1.40	2.50	n/a	n/a	n/a
K6772	3.30	1.25	n/a	n/a	n/a	n/a
Sanyo	3.00	1.15	n/a	n/a	n/a	n/a
Seiko (Mister Loaf)	3.30	1.20	2.40	3.30	3.30	n/a
Welbilt						
ABM 100	4.40	2.20	n/a	4.40	5.00	n/a
ABM 300						
ABM 350	2.15	0.50	n/a	n/a	n/a	n/a
Zojirushi	3.50	1.30	2.50	4.30	n/a	*

* a programmable cycle enables you to determine this; suggestions and instructions given in operating manual.

UNIQUE CYCLES
Hitachi HB-B201

- jam - 1.20
- rice - .52 (timer feature up to 13 hours)

National/Panasonic 100% Whole Wheat Machine

- whole wheat dough cycle - 3.15

National/Panasonic SD-BT6N & SD-BT6P

- Variety Bread (enables you to remove dough, roll and insert a filling and replace it into the machine for baking) - 4.15
- Tender Bread (For a moist, tender texture) - 5.00
- Cake/quick bread - programmable

Zojirushi

- cake/quick breads - 2.00
- jam - 1.20
- programmable cycle for rye and whole grains

TIMER FEATURE

All machines have a timer feature which enables you to place the ingredients into the pan and tell the machine when you want the bread completed. There is nothing better or easier than having fresh, hot bread first thing in the morning or waiting for you when you arrive home from work! The following information indicates the maximum amount of time available for this feature.

Unless specific models are indicated, information pertains to all models of a company.

12 Hours: DAK, Welbilt, Mister Loaf

13 Hours: Hitachi, National/Panasonic, Regal, Sanyo, Zojirushi

14 Hours: Maxim

Note: The Welbilt and DAK machines' dough cycles have a timer feature also.

WHEN TO ADD RAISINS AND SIMILAR INGREDIENTS

Raisins, nuts, dried fruits and other similar ingredients may be added to all loaves for additional variety and spicing. Some machines have a separate, selectable cycle which beeps indicating when to add these ingredients. Other machines have the beeps on the regular cycle omitting the need to select a different cycle.

Finally, a few machines do not have this feature but I am providing instructions for when to add these ingredients. As each of the machines are different I am including the approximate time into the cycle to add these ingredients. Times are for all machines by the same manufacturer unless specified. (Hours.Minutes)

DAK - 1.35+

Hitachi - .25

Maxim - at the beginning of the cycle

Mister Loaf - at the beginning of the cycle

National/Panasonic - during the rest period following the first kneading, approximately 25 minutes.

Regal - .25

Sanyo - .23   ABM 300 & ABM 350 - .25
Welbilt - ABM 100 - 1.35   Zojirushi - .35 +/-

MAXIMUM SIZE LOAF

The maximum capacity of the bread machine is important in selecting the appropriate machine for you and your family. Remember that you may always make smaller loaves than your machine's capacity. I have found, however, that due to the shape of the pan, it is better to make the manufacturer's suggested size on the National and Panasonic machines.

Please note that many machines will successfully knead and bake a larger amount of flour for a larger loaf if whole wheat, rye or other whole grains are used. If experimenting with larger amounts than your manufacturer recommends, you may overflow your pan resulting in an uncooked top, sunken top or even having to clean the inside of the machine. Do not exceed your manufacturer's recommendations with just the white bread flour.

1-pound loaf or 2 cups of flour:

Maxim BB-1   Sanyo
Mister Loaf   Seiko
Regal K6772   Welbilt ABM 300 & ABM 350

1½-pound loaf or 3+ cups of flour:

DAK   Regal Deluxe
Hitachi HB-B101 & HB-B201   Welbilt ABM 100
National/Panasonic SD-BT6N, SD-BT6P Zojirushi

COMMON QUESTIONS & ANSWERS

There are no times given in the recipes. How do I know how long to bake the bread?

One of the main features of bread machines is that you do not have to do anything other than place the ingredients in the pan, put the pan into the machine and push the button for the correct cycle. You do not set any time limits on the machines as it is all done by computer programs within the machines themselves. If you have questions on how to operate your machine, you should read the owner's manual for your particular machine. Unless otherwise specified, recipes were tested on the basic white cycle.

Can I vary the size of the loaf made?

Absolutely. If your machine makes a large loaf (1.5 lb.+ or 3-4 cups of flour), you may make any size loaf in the book. This is especially nice if you are making a loaf for just one or two people and do not require a large loaf. Also, if you are making a spice or herb bread to accompany a specific meal but do not want a large loaf, make a smaller one. If your machine's capacity is a smaller loaf to begin with (1 pound or 2 cups of flour), you may make the recipes using either 1½ cups or 2 cups of flour. Please note that a few of the recipes call for a total of 2¼ or even 2½ cups of flour. You may be able to use these recipes if the flour is a combination of white and whole wheat or other whole grains. Do not exceed your manufacturer's recommendations with all white flour. You may always decrease the size of the loaf but do not increase beyond your machine's capacity.

Why should I ever make a loaf on the dough cycle? It defeats the purpose of the machine!

The dough cycle breads do require that you remove the dough and shape it for baking in your conventual oven. Keep in mind that the machine has done the initial kneading (the hardest part of making homemade bread) and rising. If invited to a pot-luck dinner or party, it is still easier (I think) to make a beautiful coffee bread than a few dozen cookies.

I love kneading bread. Why should I buy a machine?

Many people do not want to give up the feeling of kneading the dough. In this case, any recipe may be made on the dough cycle, removed and kneaded and then baked in a conventional oven. I do not include times or temperatures for this.

Can the recipes be made by hand?

Yes, each of these recipes may be made "the old-fashioned way." However, I do not include instructions for this.

Can salt be eliminated for someone on a salt-restricted diet?

No. Salt is one of those necessities in bread. You may, however, cut the amount of salt to ⅛ - ¼ teaspoon per loaf of bread. Keep in mind that salt restricts the yeast growth; therefore, if the bread rises too high, decrease the amount of sugar also. (Sugar feeds the yeast, assisting in the rising of the dough).

Someone told me to add gluten to all my breads. Should I?

One or two tablespoons of gluten may certainly be added to any bread recipe. Gluten is usually added to recipes using whole wheat, rye or other whole grains as it contributes to a higher-rising loaf. I would not hesitate to add gluten to these recipes. It is not necessary, however, to add gluten to recipes using one hundred percent bread flour as the flour already has a high gluten content.

What is gluten?

Gluten is the ingredient in the flour which, when combined with the yeast, allows the dough to rise. Bread flour has a higher gluten content than all-purpose flour which will give a higher loaf. Whole wheat, rye and other grains have a lower gluten content which is why they are often smaller loaves. If you will refer to my first book, **The Bread Machine Cookbook**, you will find a lengthy analysis of bread ingredients.

I have a gluten intolerance. Do you have recipes for gluten-free breads?

Ener-G Foods in Seattle has information available for gluten-free breads. See *Sources* in the back of the book.

The recipes in your book use dried herbs. How much should I use if I want to use fresh herbs?

As a general rule, if you use fresh herbs, you should use three times the amount of dried herbs the recipe calls for.

Some ingredients are seasonal. Do you recommend substitutions?

Substitutions may be made for certain ingredients. For example, I often use dry mixed fruit bits in place of citron or chopped almonds in place of slivered almonds. Hitachi suggests substituting Zamphiam or Celeous for gluten. Milk or buttermilk may be substituted for the water or vice versa.

May I use egg substitutes in order to cut down on cholesterol?

Absolutely. Amounts have been provided in each recipe.

Can dry milk be used in place of fresh milk?

This is very common especially when using the timer cycle or when out of or low on fresh milk. Replace the milk with water, cup for cup, and add the dry milk (about one to four tablespoons depending on the size of the loaf and the amount of "milk" used).

Should I use whole wheat bread flour or is the whole wheat all-purpose flour okay?

Whole wheat bread flour has a higher gluten content than whole wheat all purpose flour which will result in a higher-rising loaf. Either may be used, or use whole wheat all-purpose flour and add about one tablespoon of gluten per cup, if desired. Both whole wheat bread flour and gluten may be purchased either through your health food store or from one of the sources listed on page 167.

My yeast doesn't always work — why?

Open containers or packages of yeast should always be tightly sealed and refrigerated. Personally, I use either one half a package (plus or minus) per loaf or the measured teaspoon of a bulk yeast — available in your grocery store in a jar or from a health food store in the refrigerated section. Bring the measured yeast to room temperature before using. I often let the pan with all the ingredients in it sit for about five minutes before starting the machine.

How do you use ½ egg?

I find it helpful to use egg substitutes (found in the frozen section of the grocery stores) for partial eggs. To help determine how much to use, I have listed the equivalent egg substitutions along with each recipe.

Your recipes call for ⅓ teaspoon and I cannot find one. What should I do?

The following should help in determining "hard to find" measuring spoons:

⅟₁₆ tsp. = one half of ⅛ tsp.

⅛ tsp. = one half of ¼ tsp.

⅓ tsp. = a heaping ¼ tsp.

⅔ tsp. = a heaping ½ tsp. or scant ¾ tsp.

½ tbs. = 1½ tsp.

1⅓ tbs. = 1 tbs. + 1 tsp.

Do recipes require adjustments for high altitudes?

You may find it necessary to adjust recipes. Some suggestions include:

Reduce yeast approximately ⅛ to ¼ teaspoon.

Reduce sugar between 1 to 3 tablespoons.

Increase liquid by 1 to 4 tablespoons.

The higher the altitude, the higher your reductions, etc. should be.

Some breads do not always cook properly — either they come out too doughy or they start to bake and then sink. What can I do?

This is a very common question and is one of the most difficult to answer. First, make sure you are not baking too large a loaf for your machine. If that is not the case, the cause is most probably humidity-related. Try cutting back, next time with the same recipe, the fat (margarine/butter/vegetable oil) and liquid amounts. Cut your liquid by ¼ of the total amount, add that in, one tablespoon at a time, as the dough is kneading until the bread forms a well rounded ball. In a worst case scenario, make your bread on days that are low in humidity and freeze a few loaves. I have found that this problem usually occurs with recipes containing either a lot of fat, fruit and/or sugar. It may not occur on all machines.

I often have trouble removing the kneading blade or paddle from the machine after the loaf is baked. What should I do?

This seems to be very common. My suggestion is to pour very hot water into the bottom of the pan and soak for about 5 minutes and then remove. Sometimes I have to "play" with the paddle, twisting it one way, while at the same time twisting the bottom of it from the outside of the pan, in the opposite direction. One breadmaker from Ithaca, NY recommends putting a very small amount of vegetable oil on the shaft prior to putting the kneading paddle in the pan. Always remove the paddle to clean your pan as you may have serious problems removing it if several layers of bread dough have baked in it. That could, I would think, result in a loss of proper kneading action.

The kneading paddle often becomes embedded in the loaf. What should I do?

Take a plastic or wooden knife or spoon handle and gently remove the paddle from the loaf. Be sure not to scratch the paddle.

When the kneading starts, sometimes the dough looks too dry or it forms "balls" like playdough. What should I do?

Some moisture in the dough is provided by the margarine/butter or other fats and this can take longer to knead into the dough than the regular liquid, causing this effect. If after 5 to 10 minutes, the dough is not one, smooth ball, you may add liquid one tablespoon at a time. While all recipes have been tested on all machines, there are variations in humidity/dryness, machine calibrations and even ingredients which may require slight adjustments.

The height and shape of the loaves sometimes differ. Why?

If loaves from the same recipe differ, it is probably due to variations in temperature (room or weather), humidity or even length of time the ingredients sit idle (i.e. on the timer). Different recipes will have different heights and shapes due to the ingredients. Whole wheat, rye and other whole grains will not rise as high as white breads. Additional ingredients such as nuts, raisins, fruits etc. will also cause the loaf to not rise as much either.

Your recipes are not large enough for my machine. I have to double them.

Some manufacturers recommend and, in fact, provide recipes for loaves larger than 1½ lbs. (3 cups). You will note that these recipes are always for a combination of white and whole wheat, rye or other whole grains. This is because the combination flours have a lower gluten content which results in a smaller rising loaf. More than three cups of white bread flour in any machine may overflow the pan. So that you need not bother checking to see the amount of flour used, I have done all the calculations for you. None of the recipes exceed four cups of combined white/whole grain flours as the bread may not bake properly in any of the machines.

Sometimes loaves have sunken tops but the same recipe works great at other times. Why?

I have found that during times of high humidity or high temperatures the loaves may have sunken tops. This is especially true if the machine is left on the timer cycle over-night. You may wish to add a tablespoon or two of flour or decrease the liquid during a period of high humidity. If using the timer cycle, you may wish to use as short a period as possible.

Why is the bread damp sometimes?

This is an indication that the bread sat in the pan too long. I generally remove the bread as soon as the machine starts the cooling cycle.

How should I cut the bread?

Most people have difficulty cutting homemade bread evenly. It is easier to cut if it is cool. However, I cannot wait that long. My recommendation is to use a serrated knife and to use a sawing action instead of pushing straight down.

Is there a special way to wrap baked bread for storage?
Wrap the loaf itself in a kitchen or tea towel and then wrap that in plastic.

Can I make dough on the dough cycle and then freeze it for later baking?
Yes, although you should not freeze the dough for more than two weeks. Shape the dough as desired, leaving plenty of room for expansion in a pan, and wrap in plastic. When ready to bake, place the frozen dough into a greased loaf pan, thaw the dough and let it rise for about four to six hours (until it overflows the pan by about ½ inch) and bake. Recipes in this book do not include times or temperatures for baking in conventional ovens.

Occasionally smoke comes out of the machine or it smells like it's burning — why?
There are probably spilled ingredients in the machine. Check the machine and clean well prior to starting each cycle.

Sometimes there is flour on the side of the loaves. Why?
Occasionally flour sticks to the side of the machine and does not knead into the loaf. During the kneading cycle you can take a rubber spatula and try to push the flour into the dough or you can leave it and brush it off the baked loaf as best as you can.

Why do loaves not cook completely?

Most probably the size of the recipe is too large. Use a smaller size next time. If this is not the case, cut back the amount of yeast used and maybe even decrease the amount of sugar and/or increase the amount of salt.

What should I do if the loaves do not rise as high as normal?

I am assuming that this question relates to a particular recipe which all of a sudden does not rise as high as it has previously. There are several possible reasons which could cause this:

Check the amount of yeast used and increase it if necessary. Make sure that the yeast is still good — you should be able to smell it to see if it is still viable. You should always check the date of expiration too!

Make sure you are using bread flour and not all-purpose flour.

The sugar and/or water may need to be increased slightly.

Occasionally you may produce a smaller loaf if the machine sits in a draft from a window or open door. I have not experienced this but have heard of it.

If you have a consistent problem with poor rising with all recipes and all loaves, you may want to have your machine's calibration checked.

Can I use the quick yeast on a regular cycle or vice versa?

No. Use the correct yeast on the correct cycle.

Why is the top poorly shaped sometimes?
This is an indication of not enough water. Try increasing it by a tablespoon or two until the dough itself is a well rounded ball.

Is it important how I place the ingredients into the pan?
Yes, all recipes are divided into wet and dry ingredients. Place them into the machine so that the liquids and the yeast do not tough each other until the machine kneads them together. This is extremely important if using the timer cycle.

May I add flour to the dough when removed from the machine to assist in rolling the dough?
Absolutely, add the flour about one tablespoon at a time just until you can easily handle the dough with no stickiness.

What are some common mistakes made?
I can share with you some mistakes I have made so that you, hopefully, can avoid them:

- Forgetting to put the yeast in.
- Losing track of how many cups of flour were put in (or any other ingredient).
- Not putting the kneading blade or paddle in correctly — the dough does

not get kneaded!

- Not putting in the kneading rod (some machines have a kneading rod in the side of the pan) — the liquid will pour out the side.
- Putting the machine on the wrong setting. If your machine does not automatically default to the standard white setting, make sure you check which cycle you use.

May I substitute bulgur for cracked wheat?

Yes, but do not soak the bulgur as you do the cracked wheat. Place it in the machine so that it does not contact the liquid, if using the timer cycle.

My dough cycle is long (over 2 hours). Can I shorten it at all?

Yes. Dak and Welbilt machine's dough cycles are long because they knead the dough twice. I have found that if you let the dough knead once, rise for about an hour and then turn off the machine, the dough still works well. This is particularly true for pizza, stromboli, calzone and similar doughs.

WHITE & CHEESE BREADS

WHITE BREAD

This is a basic, no frills white bread — low fat, sugar and sodium and really good.

	Small	Medium	Large
milk or water	½ cup	¾ cup	1 cup
vegetable oil	1 tbs.	1½ tbs.	2 tbs.
honey	1 tbs.	1½ tbs.	2 tbs.
salt	⅓ tsp.	½ tsp.	⅔ tsp.
bread flour	1½ cup	2¼ cups	3 cups
yeast	1 tsp.	1½ tsp.	2½ tsp.

RICE BREAD

A delicious twist on white bread. Makes good sandwiches.

	Small	Medium	Large
cooked rice	½ cup	⅔ cup	1 cup
water	½ cup	⅔ cup	1 cup
margarine/butter	2 tsp.	1 tbs.	1⅓ tbs.
salt	¼ tsp.	⅓ tsp.	½ tsp.
sugar	¼ tsp.	⅓ tsp.	½ tsp.
bread flour	1½ cups	2 cups	3 cups
yeast	1 tsp.	1½ tsp.	2½ tsp.

Note: Any type of rice may be used for different flavors of bread, such as brown, wild, basmati, white, etc. Rice doubles in volume when cooked. For example, cook ¼ cup of rice grains in ½ cup of water to obtain ½ cup of cooked rice — or just use leftover rice.

COLA BREAD

This is a very easy, unique bread which picks up the flavor of whatever cola you use.

	Small	**Medium**	**Large**
cola	½ cup+1 tbs.	⅔ cup+1½ tbs.	1⅛ cups
margarine/butter	1 tbs.	1½ tbs.	2 tbs.
bread flour	1½ cups	2 cups	3 cups
yeast	1 tsp.	1½ tsp.	2½ tsp.

Use any type of soda, diet or regular; any flavor such as cherry, orange, regular cola or gingerale, etc.

SEMOLINA BREAD

Thought of in this country as a pasta flour, semolina also makes delicious bread. You'll find the color slightly yellow and the taste, nutty. A super sandwich bread.

	Small	Medium	Large
water	⅔ cup	1 cup	1⅓ cups
olive oil	2 tsp.	1 tbs.	1⅓ tbs.
salt	½ tsp.	¾ tsp.	1 tsp.
sugar	½ tsp.	¾ tsp.	1 tsp.
semolina flour	½ cup	¾ cup	1 cup
bread flour	1½ cups	2¼ cups	3 cups
yeast	1 tsp.	1½ tsp.	2 tsp.

CHEESE BREAD

A rich, absolutely wonderful cheese bread.

	Small	**Medium**	**Large**
water	3 tbs.	4½ tbs.	6 tbs.
eggs	2	3	4
margarine/butter	4 tbs.	6 tbs.	8 tbs.
grated cheese*	½ cup	¾ cup	1 cup
sugar	⅓ tsp.	½ tsp.	⅔ tsp.
salt	⅓ tsp.	½ tsp.	⅔ tsp.
bread flour	1½ cups	2¼ cup	3 cups
yeast	1 tsp.	1½ tsp.	2 tsp.

*Suggested cheeses: Gruyére, Swiss or a sharp cheddar

DAK, Welbilt ABM 100, and Mister Loaf - use *Sweet Bread Cycle*.

CHEDDAR CHEESE AND BACON

Make sure you make the largest loaf your machine will allow — it will go fast! Fresh bacon is preferable to bacon bits, although they may be used. If you use bacon bits, be sure to use those made from real bacon.

	Small	**Medium**	**Large**
milk	½ cup	⅔ cup	1 cup
margarine/butter	2 tsp.	1 tbs.	1⅓ tbs.
sugar	1½ tsp.	2 tsp.	1 tbs.
salt	¼ tsp.	⅓ tsp.	½ tsp.
bread flour	1½ cups	2 cups	3 cups
yeast	1 tsp.	1½ tsp.	2½ tsp.

Raisin Bread Cycle At beep add: (If National/Panasonic, add following first kneading; if Maxim or Mister Loaf, add at beginning.)

shredded cheddar cheese	⅓ cup	½ cup	⅔ cup
cooked, crumbled bacon	⅓ cup	½ cup	⅔ cup

CHEESE HERB BREAD

Wonderful with a fish or chicken dinner or for a picnic lunch. For a variation, use grated cheddar or a combination of cheddar and Swiss.

	Small	Medium	Large
water	⅔ cup	1 cup	1⅓ cups
margarine/butter	1 tbs.	1½ tbs.	2 tbs.
grated Swiss cheese	⅓ cup	½ cup	⅔ cup
salt	¼ tsp.	⅓ tsp.	½ tsp.
sugar	1½ tsp.	2¼ tsp.	3 tsp.
grated Parmesan cheese	2 tbs.	3 tbs.	¼ cup
basil	¼ tsp.	⅓ tsp.	½ tsp.
parsley	⅓ tsp.	½ tsp.	⅔ tsp.
whole wheat bread	½ cup	¾ cup	1 cup
bread flour	1½ cups	2¼ cups	3 cups
yeast	1 tsp.	1½ tsp.	2½ tsp.

JALAPEÑO CHEESE BREAD

A must for jalapeño lovers. Serve with a Mexican type meal for an instant success.

	Small	Medium	Large
milk	½ cup	⅔ cup	1 cup
margarine/butter	1 tbs.	1½ tbs.	2 tbs.
diced jalapeños	1	1½	2
grated jalapeño cheese	⅓ cup	½ cup	⅔ cup
salt	¼ tsp.	⅓ tsp.	½ tsp.
sugar	1½ tsp.	2 tsp.	3 tsp.
bread flour	1½ cups	2 cups	3 cups
yeast	1 tsp.	1½ tsp.	2½ tsp.

WINE AND CHEESE BREAD

Terrific with cheese as appetizers. I much prefer white wine although red may be used also.

	Small	Medium	Large
wine	½ cup	¾ cup	1 cup
sharp cheddar cheese, shredded	⅓ cup	½ cup	⅔ cup
margarine/butter	1 tbs.	1½ tbs.	2 tbs.
salt	⅓ tsp.	½ tsp.	⅔ tsp.
sugar	½ tsp.	¾ tsp.	1 tsp.
bread flour	1½ cups	2¼ cups	3 cups
yeast	1 tsp.	1½ tsp.	2 tsp.

QUICK SOUR

I received several requests for a "salt-rise" bread but did not have any luck in developing one. This alternative is an easy, no fuss way to enjoy sourdough.

	Small	Medium	Large
Starter*:			
water	½ cup	⅔ cup	1 cup
bread flour	½ cup	⅔ cup	1 cup
sugar	⅛ tsp.	⅛ tsp.	¼ tsp.
yeast	1 tsp.	1½ tsp.	2 tsp.

Stir ingredients together in the order given, cover with plastic and let sit in a warm location overnight or for 6 to 8 hours.

	Small	Medium	Large
starter	*see above	*see above	*see above
milk	2 tbs.	3 tbs.	¼ cup
vinegar	½ tsp.	⅔ tsp.	1 tsp.
vegetable oil	1½ tsp.	2 tsp.	1 tbs.
salt	¼ tsp.	⅓ tsp.	½ tsp.
sugar	½ tsp.	⅔ tsp.	1 tsp.
bread flour	1½ cups	2 cups	3 cups
yeast	1 tsp.	1½ tsp.	2 tsp.

WHOLE WHEAT, RYE & OTHER GRAINS

100% WHOLE WHEAT BREAD

A pure whole wheat bread will not rise as much as one which uses a combination of white and whole wheat flour. This is a delicious, wheaty bread.

	Small	Medium	Large
water	3/4 cup	1 1/8 cups	1 1/2 cups
vegetable oil	2 tsp.	1 tbs.	1 1/3 tbs.
honey	2 tbs.	3 tbs.	1/4 cup
salt	1/4 tsp.	1/3 tsp.	1/2 tsp.
whole wheat bread flour	2 cups	3 cups	4 cups
yeast	2 tsp.	2 1/2 tsp.	3 tsp.

If you have a machine which has a whole grain setting (National/Panasonic 100% Whole Wheat, Maxim, or Zojirushi's programmable cycle), use that cycle for best results. Otherwise, this loaf was tested on a regular white cycle on all other machines.

Note: If you cannot locate whole wheat bread flour, use the regular all purpose but add gluten (available in a health food store) in the following amounts:

gluten	3 tbs.	4 1/2 tbs.	6 tbs.

CLASSIC WHOLE WHEAT BREAD

A really good, basic whole wheat.

	Small	Medium	Large
water	⅔ cup	1 cup	1⅓ cups
margarine	1 tbs.	1½ tbs.	2 tbs.
salt	⅓ tsp.	½ tsp.	⅔ tsp.
brown sugar	⅔ tsp.	1 tsp.	1⅓ tsp.
whole wheat flour	1 cup	1½ cups	2 cups
bread flour	1 cup	1½ cups	2 cups
yeast	1 tsp.	1½ tsp.	2 tsp.

WHOLE WHEAT WITH BRAN

This whole wheat bread is great for sandwiches. Choose either milk or water, and either wheat or oat bran.

	Small	Medium	Large
milk/water	¾ cup	1⅛ cups	1½ cups
vegetable oil	1⅓ tbs.	2 tbs.	2⅔ tbs.
honey	1⅓ tbs.	2 tbs.	2⅔ tbs.
salt	⅓ tsps.	½ tsp.	⅔ tsp.
wheat/oat bran	¼ cup	⅓ cup	½ cup
whole wheat flour	1 cup	1½ cups	2 cups
bread flour	1 cup	1½ cups	2 cups
yeast	1 tsp.	1½ tsp.	2 tsp.

RYE BEER BREAD

A subtly different flavored loaf with a great texture. Slices well for sandwiches.

	Small	Medium	Large
beer	3/4 cup	1 1/8 cups	1 1/2 cups
vegetable oil	1 1/2 tbs.	2 1/4 tbs.	3 tbs.
sugar	1/4 tsp.	1/3 tsp.	1/2 tsp.
salt	1/4 tsp.	1/3 tsp.	1/2 tsp.
rye flour	1 cup	1 1/2 cups	2 cups
bread flour	1 cup	1 1/2 cups	2 cups
yeast	1 tsp.	1 1/2 tsp.	2 1/2 tsp.

Note: For a regular beer bread, you may substitute bread flour for the rye. Do not, however, use more than 2 or 3 cups of bread flour in your machine.

MULTI GRAIN BREAD

A hearty, low-rising loaf. Low fat with lots of nutrition. Use wheat or oat bran.

	Small	Medium	Large
water	2/3 cup	1 cup	1 1/3 cups
vegetable oil	1 tbs.	1 1/2 tbs.	2 tbs.
honey	1 tbs.	1 1/2 tbs.	2 tbs.
salt	1/3 tsp.	1/2 tsp.	2/3 tsp.
wheat germ	2 tbs.	3 tbs.	1/4 cup
wheat/oat bran	2 tbs.	3 tbs.	1/4 cup
whole wheat flour	1/4 cup	1/3 cup	1/2 cup
wheat flakes	1/4 cup	1/3 cup	1/2 cup
oat flour	1/4 cup	1/3 cup	1/2 cup
oats	1/4 cup	1/3 cup	1/2 cup
bread flour	1 cup	1 1/2 cups	2 cups
yeast	1 1/2 tsp.	2 tsp.	2 1/2 tsp.

Note: If you do not have wheat flakes, omit and double either (not both) the oats or the whole wheat flour.

MAPLE WHEAT BREAD

A tasty, sweet bread — the taste of maple syrup is delicious. For variety, substitute oak flakes for the wheat flakes and oat flour for the whole wheat flour.

	Small	**Medium**	**Large**
water	½ cup	⅔ cup	1 cup
maple syrup	⅓ cup	½ cup	⅔ cup
margarine/butter	1 tbs.	1½ tbs.	2 tbs.
salt	½ tsp.	¾ tsp.	1 tsp.
wheat flakes	½ cup	¾ cup	1 cup
whole wheat flour	½ cup	¾ cup	1 cup
bread flour	1 cup	1½ cups	2 cups
nonfat dry milk	1 tbs.	1½ tbs.	2 tbs.
yeast	1 tsp.	1½ tsp.	2 tsp.

HONEY BREAD

This bread is great whether eaten alone or in sandwiches.

	Small	Medium	Large
water	½ cup	⅔ cup	1 cup
vegetable oil	1½ tsp.	2 tsp.	1 tbs.
honey	2 tbs.	3 tbs.	¼ cup
salt	½ tsp.	¾ tsp.	1 tsp.
oatmeal	½ cup	¾ cup	1 cup
bread flour	1 cup	1¼ cups	2 cups
yeast	1 tsp.	1½ tsp.	2½ tsp.

WHOLE WHEAT CINNAMON RAISIN NUT BREAD

This is particularly good toasted. Wonderful for either breakfast or sand-wiches. Choose either wheat or oat bran and flakes.

	Small	Medium	Large
milk or water	⅔ cup	1 cup	1⅓ cups
margarine/butter	1 tbs.	1½ tbs.	2 tbs.
brown sugar	1 tbs.	1½ tbs.	2 tbs.
salt	¼ tsp.	⅓ tsp.	½ tsp.
cinnamon	½ tsp.	¾ tsp.	1 tsp.
wheat/oat bran	¼ cup	⅓ cup	½ cup
wheat/oat flakes	½ cup	¾ cup	1 cup
whole wheat flour	½ cup	¾ cup	1 cup
bread flour	1 cup	1½ cups	2 cups
yeast	1½ tsp.	2 tsp.	2½ tsp.

Raisin Bread Cycle   At beep add: (If National/Panasonic, add following first kneading; if Maxim or Mister Loaf, add at beginning.)

	Small	Medium	Large
raisins	⅓ cup	½ cup	⅔ cup
chopped walnuts/pecans	⅓ cup	½ cup	⅔ cup

GRANOLA BREAD

Use your favorite granola cereal for a wonderful change-of-pace.

	Small	Medium	Large
milk/water	½ cup	¾ cup	1 cup
vegetable oil	1⅓ tbs.	2 tbs.	2⅔ tbs.
honey	1⅓ tbs.	2 tbs.	2⅔ tbs.
salt	⅓ tsp.	½ tsp.	⅔ tsp.
grated orange peel	½ tsp.	¾ tsp.	1 tsp.
granola cereal	1 cup	1½ cups	2 cups
bread flour	1 cup	1½ cups	2 cups
yeast	1 tsp.	1½ tsp.	2 tsp.

Raisin Bread Cycle At beep add: (If National/Panasonic, add following first kneading; if Maxim or Mister Loaf, add at beginning.)

	Small	Medium	Large
raisins, optional	¼ cup	⅓ cup	½ cup
sunflower seeds, optional	¼ cup	⅓ cup	½ cup

CRACKED WHEAT OAT BREAD

A wonderful variation on cracked wheat. Nice nutty taste and texture. Wheat flakes may be substituted for cracked wheat for a delicious variation.

	Small	Medium	Large
water	⅔ cup	1 cup	1⅓ cups
vegetable oil	1½ tbs.	2¼ tbs.	3 tbs.
honey	1 tbs.	1½ tbs.	2 tbs.
cracked wheat	½ cup	¾ cup	1 cup
salt	¼ tsp.	⅓ tsp.	½ tsp.
oats	½ cup	¾ cup	1 cup
bread flour	1 cup	1½ cups	2 cups
yeast	1 tsp.	1½ tsp.	2 tsp.

The cracked wheat must sit in the liquid for at least one hour. I usually make this bread on the timer cycle on all machines except the National/Panasonic, DAK or Welbilts. In these machines, measure your water and cracked wheat and soak prior to inserting into the machines.

CRACKED WHEAT ALMOND BREAD

This is soon to be one of your favorites, as it is at my house. Wheat flakes may be substituted for the cracked wheat for a delicious variation.

	Small	Medium	Large
water	⅔ cup	1 cup	1⅓ cups
cracked wheat	½ cup	¾ cup	1 cup
margarine/butter	2 tbs.	3 tbs.	¼ cup
brown sugar	1 tbs.	1½ tbs.	2 tbs.
salt	½ tsp.	¾ tsp.	1 tsp.
whole wheat flour	½ cup	¾ cup	1 cup
bread flour	1 cup	1½ cups	2 cups
nonfat dry milk	2 tbs.	3 tbs.	¼ cup
yeast	1 tsp.	1½ tsp.	2 tsp.

Raisin Bread Cycle   At beep add: (If National/Panasonic, add following first kneading; if Maxim or Mister Loaf, add at beginning.)

chopped almonds	½ cup	¾ cup	1 cup

Note: See page 42 for instructions about soaking cracked wheat.

HONEY WHEAT BERRY

An absolutely wonderful bread. The honey-soaked wheat berries are a terrific addition to this nutritious bread.

	Small	Medium	Large
soaked wheat berries	*see page 45	*see page 45	*see page 45
water	½ cup	⅔ cup	1 cup
vegetable oil	1½ tsp.	2 tsp.	1 tbs.
honey	2 tbs.	3 tbs.	¼ cup
salt	½ tsp.	¾ tsp.	1 tsp.
wheat germ	1½ tbs.	2¼ tbs.	3 tbs.
whole wheat flour	⅔ cup	1 cup	1⅓ cups
bread flour	1 cup	1½ cups	2 cups
nonfat dry milk	2 tbs.	3 tbs.	¼ cup
yeast	1 tsp.	1½ tsp.	2½ tsp.

Soaked wheat berries

	Small	Medium	Large
wheat berries	⅓ cup	½ cup	⅔ cup
water	1 cup	1½ cups	2 cups
honey	1½ tbs.	2 tbs.	3 tbs.

Combine ingredients in a saucepan and boil for approximately 1 hour, stirring occasionally (add water if necessary). Remove from heat, cover and let stand 6 to 12 hours (all day or overnight). Drain any standing water before adding the berries to the dough.

WALNUT RYE

You will love this absolutely superb combination of rye and walnuts.

	Small	**Medium**	**Large**
milk or water	¾ cup	1¼ cups	1½ cups
walnut oil	2 tbs.	3 tbs.	¼ cup
salt	⅔ tsp.	1 tsp.	1⅓ tsp.
sugar	⅔ tsp.	1 tsp.	1⅓ tsp.
whole wheat flour	½ cup	¾ cup	1 cup
rye flour	½ cup	¾ cup	1 cup
bread flour	1 cup	1½ cups	2 cups
yeast	1½ tsp.	2 tsp.	2½ tsp.

Raisin Bread Cycle   At beep add: (If National/Panasonic, add following first kneading; if Maxim or Mister Loaf, add at beginning.)

chopped walnuts	½ cup	¾ cup	1 cup

RAISIN PUMPERNICKEL

Raisins are a delicious addition to this pumpernickel - great with cream cheese.

	Small	Medium	Large
water	¾ cup	1⅛ cups	1½ cups
vegetable oil	1 tbs.	1½ tbs.	2 tbs.
molasses	1 tbs.	1½ tbs.	2 tbs.
unsweetened cocoa	1 tbs.	1½ tbs.	2 tbs.
salt	¼ tsp.	⅓ tsp.	½ tsp.
instant coffee granules	½ tsp.	¾ tsp.	1 tsp.
caraway seeds	2 tsp.	1 tbs.	1⅓ tbs.
cornmeal	¼ cup	⅓ cup	½ cup
rye flour	¾ cup	1¼ cups	1½ cups
bread flour	1 cup	1½ cups	2 cups
yeast	1½ tsp.	2 tsp.	2½ tsp.

Raisin Bread Cycle At beep add: (If National/Panasonic, add following first kneading; if Maxim or Mister Loaf, add at beginning.)

raisins	⅓ cup	½ cup	⅔ cup

WHOLE WHEAT RAISIN OATMEAL

A great combination of whole wheat, oatmeal and raisins.

	Small	Medium	Large
water	2/3 cup	1 cup	1 1/3 cups
vegetable oil	1 tbs.	1 1/2 tbs.	2 tbs.
honey	1 tbs.	1 1/2 tbs.	2 tbs.
salt	1/3 tsp.	1/2 tsp.	2/3 tsp.
oats	1/2 cup	3/4 cup	1 cup
whole wheat flour	1/2 cup	3/4 cup	1 cup
bread flour	1 cup	1 1/2 cups	2 cups
yeast	1 tsp.	1 1/2 tsp.	2 tsp.

Raisin Bread Cycle   At beep add: (If National/Panasonic, add following first kneading; if Maxim or Mister Loaf, add at beginning.)

	Small	Medium	Large
raisins	1/3 cup	1/2 cup	2/3 cup
chopped nuts, optional	1/3 cup	1/2 cup	2/3 cup

RYE CORNMEAL BREAD

Rye and cornmeal make a delicious combination.

	Small	Medium	Large
water	⅔ cup	1 cup	1⅓ cups
vegetable oil	1 tbs.	1½ tbs.	2 tbs.
molasses	1½ tbs.	2¼ tbs.	3 tbs.
salt	¼ tsp.	⅓ tsp.	½ tsp.
rye flour	½ cup	¾ cup	1 cup
cornmeal	½ cup	¾ cup	1 cup
bread flour	1 cup	1½ cups	2 cups
yeast	1½ tsp.	2 tsp.	2½ tsp.

RAISIN RYE

This bread is particularly good with cream cheese.

	Small	Medium	Large
water	⅔ cup	1 cup	1⅓ cups
vegetable oil	1 tbs.	1½ tbs.	2 tbs.
molasses	1¼ tbs.	1¾ tbs.	2½ tbs.
salt	⅓ tsp.	½ tsp.	⅔ tsp.
unsweetened cocoa	1 tbs.	1½ tbs.	2 tbs.
caraway seeds, optional	2 tsp.	1 tbs.	1⅓ tbs.
rye flour	1 cup	1½ cups	2 cups
bread flour	1 cup	1½ cups	2 cups
yeast	1½ tsp.	2 tsp.	2½ tsp.

Raisin Bread Cycle   At beep add: (If National/Panasonic, add following first kneading; if Maxim or Mister Loaf, add at beginning.)

raisins	⅓ cup	½ cup	⅔ cup

FOUR SEED BREAD

The seeds add lots of flavor — really good.

	Small	Medium	Large
milk/water	⅔ cup	1 cup	1⅓ cups
vegetable oil	1⅓ tbs.	2 tbs.	2⅔ tbs.
honey	1⅓ tbs.	2 tbs.	2⅔ tbs.
salt	⅓ tsp.	½ tsp.	⅔ tsp.
fennel seeds	½ tsp.	¾ tsp.	1 tsp.
caraway seeds	½ tsp.	¾ tsp.	1 tsp.
anise seeds	½ tsp.	¾ tsp.	1 tsp.
celery seeds	½ tsp.	¾ tsp.	1 tsp.
whole wheat flour	1 cup	1½ cups	2 cups
bread flour	1 cup	1½ cups	2 cups
yeast	1 tsp.	1½ tsp.	2 tsp.

KASHA BREAD

A hearty, flavorful bread. Put the raisins in at the beginning so that they become crushed — unless you have a Maxim or Mister Loaf, in which case you will have whole raisins for a slightly different, but equally delicious bread.

	Small	Medium	Large
water	3/4 cup	1 1/8 cups	1 1/2 cups
vegetable oil	1 1/3 tbs.	2 tbs.	2 2/3 tbs.
salt	2/3 tsp.	1 tsp.	1 1/3 tsp.
buckwheat groats	1/4 cup	1/3 cup	1/2 cup
whole wheat flour	3/4 cup	1 cup	1 1/2 cups
bread flour	1 cup	1 2/3 cups	2 cups
raisins	1/4 cup	1/3 cup	1/2 cup
yeast	1 tsp.	1 1/2 tsp.	2 1/2 tsp.

QUICK SOUR RYE

A delicious, dense loaf.

	Small	Medium	Large
Starter*:			
water	¾ cup	1⅛ cups	1½ cups
rye flour	1 cup	1½ cups	2 cups
yeast	1 tsp.	1½ tsp.	2 tsp.

Place ingredients in pan and allow machine to knead once. Turn off machine (reset button or unplug) and allow dough to sit overnight or for 6-8 hours. The sponge will smell a little sour.

	Small	Medium	Large
starter	*see above	*see above	*see above
vegetable oil	1 tbs.	1½ tbs.	2 tbs.
honey	1 tbs.	1½ tbs.	2 tbs.
salt	¼ tsp.	⅓ tsp.	½ tsp.
caraway seeds	2 tsp.	1 tbs.	1⅓ tbs.
bread flour	1 cup	1½ cups	2 cups
yeast	1 tsp.	1½ tsp.	2 tsp.

VEGETABLE & FRUIT BREADS

ORANGE BREAD

Delicious — great for breakfast. Make sure the mandarin orange segments are tightly packed in the measuring cup.

	Small	Medium	Large
mandarin orange segments	⅔ cup	1 cup	1⅓ cups
margarine	1 tbs.	1½ tbs.	2 tbs.
orange juice concentrate	1 tbs.	1½ tbs.	2 tbs.
sugar	2 tbs.	3 tbs.	¼ cup
salt	½ tsp.	⅔ tsp.	1 tsp.
bread flour	1½ cups	2 cups	3 cups
yeast	1 tsp.	1½ tsp.	2 tsp.

Welbilt ABM 100, DAK and Mister Loaf - use *Sweet Bread Cycle.*

BERRY BREAD

This recipe may really use any berry or berry syrup — choose your favorites. Try it with cranberries in the fall and substitute honey for the berry syrup. If cranberries are fresh, add ⅓ ½ ⅔ cups water and syrup of your choice.

	Small	**Medium**	**Large**
raspberries	⅔ cups	1 cup	1⅓ cups
vegetable oil	1 tbs.	1½ tbs.	2 tbs.
raspberry syrup	2½ tbs.	3¾ tbs.	5 tbs.
salt	⅓ tsp.	½ tsp.	⅔ tsp.
whole wheat flour	1 cup	1½ cups	2 cups
bread flour	1 cup	1½ cups	2 cups
yeast	1 tsp.	1½ tsp.	2 tsp.

Raisin Bread Cycle At beep add: (If Panasonic/National, add following first kneading; if Maxim or Mister Loaf, add at beginning.)

chopped walnuts/ pecans, optional	¼ cup	⅓ cup	½ cup

Welbilt ABM 100, DAK and Mister Loaf - use *Sweet Bread Cycle*

PEACH BREAD

A great way to use fresh peaches, although canned do nicely too. Puree peeled fresh or rinsed canned peaches in a food processor or blender.

	Small	Medium	Large
peach puree	¾ cup	1⅛ cups	1½ cups
vegetable oil	1 tbs.	1½ tbs.	2 tbs.
honey	1 tbs.	1½ tbs.	2 tbs.
eggs	1	1½	2
salt	⅓ tsp.	½ tsp.	⅔ tsp.
cinnamon	⅛ tsp.	⅛ tsp.	¼ tsp.
whole wheat flour	1 cup	1½ cups	2 cups
bread flour	1 cup	1½ cups	2 cups
yeast	1 tsp.	1½ tsp.	2½ tsp.

Raisin Bread Cycle   At beep add: (If National/Panasonic, add following first kneading; if Maxim or Mister Loaf, add at beginning.)

	Small	Medium	Large
diced dried peaches	⅓ cup	½ cup	⅔ cup
figs, raisins or dates, optional	⅓ cup	½ cup	⅔ cup
egg substitute	¼ cup	6 tbs.	½ cup

HAWAIIAN MACADAMIA NUT BREAD

This superb bread will receive rave reviews. The macadamia nuts give it a wonderful flavor. You can substitute Mauna Lài™ or similar juice for the water.

	Small	Medium	Large
water	½ cup	¾ cup	1 cup
eggs	1	1½	2
margarine/butter	1 tbs.	1½ tbs.	2 tbs.
sugar	2 tbs.	3 tbs.	¼ cup
salt	⅓ tsp.	½ tsp.	⅔ tsp.
bread flour	1½ cups	2¼ cups	3 cups
nonfat dry milk	2 tbs.	3 tbs.	¼ cup
yeast	1 tsp.	1½ tsp.	2 tsp.

Raisin Bread Cycle At beep add: (If National/Panasonic, add following first kneading; if Maxim or Mister Loaf, add at beginning.)

	Small	Medium	Large
macadamia nuts, chopped	½ cup	¾ cup	1 cup
egg substitute	¼ cup	6 tbs.	½ cup

BANANA COCONUT AND MACADAMIA BREAD

This has become one of my favorites — a great tropical combination. A "must try." Vanilla extract may be substituted for the coconut extract.

	Small	Medium	Large
mashed banana	2/3 cup	1 cup	1 1/3 cups
vegetable oil	1 tbs.	1 1/2 tbs.	2 tbs.
honey	1 tbs.	1 1/2 tbs.	2 tbs.
coconut extract	1 tsp.	1 1/2 tsp.	2 tsp.
salt	1/2 tsp.	3/4 tsp.	1 tsp.
grated lemon peel	1/2 tsp.	3/4 tsp.	1 tsp.
coconut flakes	1/2 cup	3/4 cup	1 cup
whole wheat flour	3/4 cup	1 1/8 cups	1 1/2 cups
bread flour	1 cup	1 1/2 cups	2 cups
yeast	1 tsp.	1 1/2 tsp.	2 tsp.

Raisin Bread Cycle   At beep add: (If National/Panasonic, add following first kneading; if Maxim or Mister Loaf, add at beginning.)

macadamia nuts,			
chopped	1/3 cup	1/2 cup	2/3 cup

Welbilt ABM 100, DAK and Mister Loaf - use *Sweet Bread Cycle*.

DATE NUT BREAD

This dark colored, flavorful loaf of bread will have you going back for more. You'll love this even if you think you don't like dates!

	Small	Medium	Large
water	¾ cup	1⅛ cups	1½ cups
vegetable oil	1⅓ tbs.	2 tbs.	2⅔ tbs.
molasses	⅔ tbs.	1 tbs.	1⅓ tbs.
salt	⅔ tsp.	1 tsp.	1⅓ tsp
unsweetened cocoa	1⅓ tbs.	2 tbs.	2⅔ tbs.
whole wheat flour	1 cup	1½ cups	2 cups
bread flour	1 cup	1½ cups	2 cups
yeast	1 tsp.	1½ tsp.	2½ tsp.

Raisin Bread Cycle At beep add: (If National/Panasonic, add following first kneading; if Maxim or Mister Loaf, add at beginning.)

	Small	Medium	Large
chopped dates	2½ tbs.	¼ cup	5 tbs.
chopped walnuts	2½ tbs.	¼ cup	5 tbs.

RAISIN NUT COCOA BREAD

A must for chocolate lovers. A wonderful change-of-pace raisin bread.

	Small	Medium	Large
milk/water	7/8 cup	1 1/4 cups	1 2/3 cups
margarine/butter	1 tbs.	1 1/2 tbs.	2 tbs.
salt	1/4 tsp.	1/3 tsp.	1/2 tsp.
brown sugar	2 tbs.	3 tbs.	1/4 cup
unsweetened cocoa	1 tbs.	1 1/2 tbs.	2 tbs.
oatmeal	1/2 cup	3/4 cup	1 cup
whole wheat flour	1/2 cup	3/4 cup	1 cup
bread flour	1 cup	1 1/2 cups	2 cups
yeast	1 tsp.	1 1/2 tsp.	2 tsp.

Raisin Bread Cycle At beep add: (If National/Panasonic, add following first kneading; if Maxim or Mister Loaf, add at beginning.)

	Small	Medium	Large
raisins	1/3 cup	1/2 cup	2/3 cup
chopped walnuts	1/3 cup	1/2 cup	2/3 cup

WALNUT RAISIN BREAD

Try this toasted for breakfast and you'll be hooked. Any vegetable oil may be used in place of the walnut oil.

	Small	**Medium**	**Large**
milk	2/3 cup	1 cup	1 1/3 cups
walnut oil	1 tbs.	1 1/2 tbs.	2 tbs.
honey	1 tbs.	1 1/2 tbs.	2 tbs.
salt	1/2 tsp.	3/4 tsp.	1 tsp.
whole wheat flour	1 cup	1 1/2 cups	2 cups
bread flour	1 cup	1 1/2 cups	2 cups
yeast	1 1/2 tsp.	2 tsp.	2 1/2 tsp.

Raisin Bread Cycle   At beep add: (If National/Panasonic, add following first kneading; if Maxim or Mister Loaf, add at beginning.)

	Small	Medium	Large
raisins	1/3 cup	1/2 cup	2/3 cup
chopped walnuts	1/3 cup	1/2 cup	2/3 cup

VEGETABLE BREAD

What a great way to "hide" vegetables from finicky eaters!

	Small	Medium	Large
water	¾ cup	1⅛ cups	1½ cups
margarine/butter	1 tbs.	1½ tbs.	2 tbs.
grated carrots	¼ cup	⅓ cup	½ cup
salt	⅓ tsp.	½ tsp.	⅔ tsp.
sugar	½ tsp.	¾ tsp.	1 tsp.
celery seeds	1 tsp.	1½ tsp.	2 tsp.
whole wheat flour	1 cup	1½ cups	2 cups
bread flour	1 cup	1½ cups	2 cups
yeast	1 tsp.	1½ tsp.	2½ tsp.

Raisin Bread Cycle   At beep add: (If Panasonic/National, add following first kneading; if Maxim or Mister Loaf, add at beginning.)

diced dried tomatoes, optional	¼ cup	⅓ cup	½ cup
diced bell peppers, optional	¼ cup	⅓ cup	½ cup

CORNY BREAD

This is based on my father's recipe which he devised using corn scraped off the cob. A delicious twist on cornmeal.

	Small	**Medium**	**Large**
creamed corn	¾ cup	1⅛ cups	1½ cups
vegetable oil	1 tbs.	1½ tbs.	2 tbs.
vanilla extract	½ tsp.	¾ tsp.	1 tsp.
salt	⅓ tsp.	½ tsp.	⅔ tsp.
brown sugar	1 tbs.	1½ tbs.	2 tbs.
nutmeg	⅓ tsp.	½ tsp.	⅔ tsp.
cornmeal	½ cup	¾ cup	1 cup
bread flour	1½ cups	2¼ cups	3 cups
yeast	1 tsp.	1½ tsp.	2 tsp.

Note: If you have fresh cooked corn, scrape off the kernels and fill measuring cup. Pour milk into the same measuring cup to equal the given creamed corn amount.

POTATO BREAD

Some people swear there is no other bread than potato bread. This is a delicious variation of white or whole wheat bread. Or, for another tasty variety, **Cheese Potato Bread**, *add grated cheddar*.*

	Small	Medium	Large
mashed potatoes	½ cup	¾ cup	1 cup
potato water	½ cup	¾ cup	1 cup
vegetable oil	1½ tbs.	2¼ tbs.	3 tbs.
salt	½ tsp.	¾ tsp.	1 tsp.
sugar	2 tsp.	1 tbs.	1⅓ tbs.
bread flour	1 cup	1½ cups	2 cups
whole wheat flour	1 cup	1½ cups	2 cups
yeast	1 tsp.	1½ tsp.	2 tsp.

Note: If you prefer an all white bread, substitute bread flour for the whole wheat flour. Do not exceed, however, 2 or 3 cups of the bread flour depending on the capacity of your machine.

*grated cheddar	¼ cup	⅓ cup	½ cup

BELL PEPPER BREAD

A hot, spicy bread. You'll find the crushed dried red pepper and the white pepper on the spice shelf at your grocers'.

	Small	Medium	Large
water	⅔ cup	1 cup	1⅓ cups
olive oil	1 tbs.	1½ tbs.	2 tbs.
salt	½ tsp.	⅔ tsp.	1 tsp.
sugar	½ tsp.	⅔ tsp.	1 tsp.
crushed dried			
red pepper	½ tsp.	⅔ tsp.	1 tsp.
white pepper	¼ tsp.	⅓ tsp.	½ tsp.
whole wheat flour	1 cup	1½ cup	2 cups
bread flour	1 cup	1½ cup	2 cups
yeast	1 tsp.	1½ tsp.	2 tsp.

Raisin Bread Cycle At beep add: (If National/Panasonic, add following first kneading; if Maxim or Mister Loaf, add at beginning.)

diced red and/or			
green bell peppers	½ cup	¾ cup	1 cup

LENTIL BREAD

What a great, tasty way to increase protein in bread. Especially good for vegetarians. Instead of lentils, try using beans from a 9- or 13-bean soup combination package, or try your favorite — kidney, black or navy.

	Small	**Medium**	**Large**
water	2/3 cup	1 cup	1 1/3 cups
cooked beans	1/2 cup	3/4 cup	1 cup
olive oil	1 tbs.	1 1/2 tbs.	2 tbs.
honey	1 tbs.	1 1/2 tbs.	2 tbs.
salt	1/2 tsp.	3/4 tsp.	1 tsp.
whole wheat flour	1 cup	1 1/2 cups	2 cups
bread flour	1 cup	1 1/2 cups	2 cups
yeast	1 tsp.	1 1/2 tsp.	2 1/2 tsp.

Cook beans according to package directions. Allow to cool to room temperature and pack tightly into measuring cup. Or use canned cooked beans, rinsed with cold water and drained.

ORANGE OATMEAL BREAD

A delicious, nutritious bread. Great for breakfast or any other time of the day.

	Small	Medium	Large
orange juice	⅔ cup	1 cup	1⅓ cups
vegetable oil	1 tbs.	1½ tbs.	2 tbs.
honey	1 tbs.	1½ tbs.	2 tbs.
salt	½ tsp.	⅔ tsp.	1 tsp.
grated orange peel	½ tsp.	¾ tsp.	1 tsp.
oats	1 cup	1½ cups	2 cups
bread flour	1 cup	1½ cups	2 cups
yeast	1 tsp.	1½ tsp.	2½ tsp.

WHOLE GRAIN ORANGE BREAD

This is a dense, hearty bread. Wonderful served with a tossed green salad with mandarin oranges, red onions and walnuts.

	Small	Medium	Large
orange juice	⅔ cup	1 cup	1⅓ cups
vegetable oil	1½ tbs.	2¼ tbs.	3 tbs.
honey	1½ tbs.	2¼ tbs.	3 tbs.
salt	⅓ tsp.	½ tsp.	⅔ tsp.
grated orange peel	1 tsp.	1½ tsp.	2 tsp.
whole wheat flour	⅓ cup	½ cup	⅔ cup
oats or oat flour	⅓ cup	½ cup	⅔ cup
rye flour	⅓ cup	½ cup	⅔ cup
bread flour	1 cup	1½ cups	2 cups
yeast	1½ tsp.	2 tsp.	2½ tsp.

Note: Oat wheat flour, available in grocery stores, may be used in place of the combined whole wheat and oat flours.

APRICOT ALMOND BREAD

An outstanding combination — a "must" for apricot lovers.

	Small	Medium	Large
milk/water	2/3 cup	1 cup	1 1/3 cups
vegetable oil	1 1/2 tbs.	2 1/4 tbs.	3 tbs.
honey	1 1/2 tbs.	2 1/4 tbs.	3 tbs.
egg	1/2	3/4	1
salt	1/3 tsp.	1/2 tsp.	2/3 tsp.
grated lemon peel	1/3 tsp.	1/2 tsp.	2/3 tsp.
whole wheat flour	1/2 cup	3/4 cup	1 cup
oats	1/2 cup	3/4 cup	1 cup
bread flour	1 cup	1 1/2 cups	2 cups
yeast	1 tsp.	1 1/2 tsp.	2 tsp.

Raisin Bread Cycle At beep add: (If National/Panasonic, add following first kneading; if Maxim or Mister Loaf, add at beginning.)

	Small	Medium	Large
diced dried apricots	1/4 cup	1/3 cup	1/2 cup
raisins	1/4 cup	1/3 cup	1/2 cup
chopped almonds	2 tbs.	3 tbs.	1/4 cup
egg substitute	2 tbs.	3 tbs.	1/4 cup

APPLE OATMEAL BREAD

This is so good it could be eaten for dessert. Try it toasted for breakfast for a great early morning treat.

	Small	**Medium**	**Large**
applesauce	⅔ cup	1 cup	1⅓ cups
vegetable oil	1 tbs.	1½ tbs.	2 tbs.
honey	1 tbs.	1½ tbs.	2 tbs.
salt	⅓ tsp.	½ tsp.	⅔ tsp.
cinnamon	¼ tsp.	⅓ tsp.	½ tsp.
oats	1 cup	1½ cups	2 cups
bread flour	1 cup	1½ cups	2 cups
yeast	1 tsp.	1½ tsp.	2 tsp.

Raisin Bread Cycle   At beep add: (If National/Panasonic, add following first kneading; if Maxim or Mister Loaf, add at beginning.)

diced dried apples	¼ cup	⅓ cup	½ cup

APPLE OATMEAL RAISIN

An wonderful breakfast bread — I like it toasted. And good for sandwiches.

	Small	Medium	Large
apple juice	2⁄3 cup	1 cup	1 1⁄3 cups
margarine/butter	1 tbs.	1 1⁄2 tbs.	2 tbs.
salt	1⁄2 tsp.	3⁄4 tsp.	1 tsp.
cinnamon	1⁄4 tsp.	1⁄3 tsp.	1⁄2 tsp.
brown sugar	1 tbs.	1 1⁄2 tbs.	2 tbs.
oat bran	2 tbs.	3 tbs.	1⁄4 cup
oats	1 cup	1 1⁄2 cups	2 cups
bread flour	1 cup	1 1⁄2 cups	2 cups
yeast	1 tsp.	1 1⁄2 tsp.	2 tsp.

Raisin Bread Cycle   At beep add: (If National/Panasonic, add following first kneading; if Maxim or Mister Loaf, add at beginning.)

	Small	Medium	Large
raisins	1⁄3 cup	1⁄2 cup	2⁄3 cup
diced fresh apples	1⁄3 cup	1⁄2 cup	2⁄3 cup
chopped nuts, optional	1⁄4 cup	1⁄3 cup	1⁄2 cup

APPLE CARROT BREAD

A great way to sneak those carrots in for finicky eaters! Delicious.

	Small	Medium	Large
apple juice	2/3 cup	1 cup	1 1/3 cups
grated carrots	1/4 cup	1/3 cup	1/2 cup
vegetable oil	1 tbs.	1 1/2 tbs.	2 tbs.
honey	1 tbs.	1 1/2 tbs.	2 tbs.
salt	1/3 tsp.	1/2 tsp.	2/3 tsp.
whole wheat flour	1 cup	1 1/2 cups	2 cups
bread flour	1 cup	1 1/2 cups	2 cups
yeast	1 tsp.	1 1/2 tsp.	2 tsp.

Raisin Bread Cycle   At beep add: (If National/Panasonic, add following first kneading; if Maxim or Mister Loaf, add at beginning.)

	Small	Medium	Large
diced dried apples	1/4 cup	1/3 cup	1/2 cup
raisins, optional	1/3 cup	1/2 cup	2/3 cup
chopped nuts, optional	1/3 cup	1/2 cup	2/3 cup

CARROT, CHERRIES AND COCONUT BREAD

You'll soon love this too — serve it as a dessert, or if you are really decadent, toasted for breakfast. Regular milk may be substituted for the coconut milk, which I usually find in the juice or baking section of the grocery store.

	Small	Medium	Large
coconut milk	½ cup	⅔ cup	1 cup
vegetable oil	2 tbs.	2½ tbs.	¼ cup
grated carrots	¼ cup	⅓ cup	½ cup
chopped maraschino cherries	8	12	16
salt	½ tsp.	⅔ tsp.	1 tsp.
sugar	1 tbs.	1⅓ tbs.	2 tbs.
flaked coconut	2 tbs.	2½ tbs.	¼ cup
cinnamon	¼ tsp.	⅓ tsp.	½ tsp.
bread flour	1½ cups	2 cups	3 cups
yeast	1 tsp.	1½ tsp.	2½ tsp.

Raisin Bread Cycle At beep add: (If National/Panasonic, add following first kneading; if Maxim or Mister Loaf, add at beginning.)

chopped walnuts	¼ cup	⅓ cup	½ cup

CARROT PINEAPPLE BREAD

For this interesting, delicious bread I use canned pineapple, well drained.

	Small	Medium	Large
water	¼ cup	⅓ cup	½ cup
crushed pineapple	½ cup	¾ cup	1 cup
grated carrot	⅓ cup	½ cup	⅔ cup
margarine/butter	1 tbs.	1½ tbs.	2 tbs.
vanilla extract	½ tsp.	¾ tsp.	1 tsp.
salt	⅓ tsp.	½ tsp.	⅔ tsp.
brown sugar	1 tbs.	1½ tbs.	2 tbs.
oats	½ cup	¾ cup	1 cup
whole wheat flour	½ cup	¾ cup	1 cup
bread flour	1 cup	1½ cups	2 cups
yeast	1 tsp.	1½ tsp.	2 tsp.

Raisin Bread Cycle   Optional — at beep add: (If National/Panasonic, add following first kneading; if Maxim or Mister Loaf, add at beginning.)

	Small	Medium	Large
chopped nuts	¼ cup	⅓ cup	½ cup
raisins	¼ cup	⅓ cup	½ cup

Welbilt ABM 100, DAK and Mister Loaf - use *Sweet Bread Cycle*

PEANUT BUTTER BANANA BREAD

This delightful bread slices well and is great for sandwiches. Try it toasted with banana slices on top for a wonderful early-morning treat.

	Small	**Medium**	**Large**
ripe mashed bananas	¾ cup	1⅛ cups	1½ cups
peanut butter	¼ cup	⅜ cup	½ cup
eggs	¾	1	1¼
salt	½ tsp.	¾ tsp.	1 tsp.
sugar	2 tbs.	3 tbs.	¼ cup
whole wheat flour	1 cup	1½ cups	2 cups
bread flour	1 cup	1½ cups	2 cups
yeast	1 tsp.	1½ tsp.	2½ tsp.

Note: ⅜ cup equals 6 tbs. or ¼ cup+2 tbs.

egg substitute	3 tbs.	¼ cup	5 tbs.

PEANUT BUTTER CHOCOLATE CHIP BREAD

Use that favorite candy bar combination in a really different dessert bread.

	Small	Medium	Large
milk	¾ cup	1⅛ cups	1½ cups
peanut butter	⅓ cup	½ cup	⅔ cup
honey	1 tbs.	1½ tbs.	2 tbs.
salt	⅓ tsp.	½ tsp.	⅔ tsp.
whole wheat flour	1 cup	1½ cups	2 cups
bread flour	1 cup	1½ cups	2 cups
yeast	1 tsp.	1½ tsp.	2 tsp.

Raisin Bread Cycle At beep add: (If National/Panasonic, add following first kneading; if Maxim or Mister Loaf, add at beginning.)

chocolate chips	⅓ cup	½ cup	⅔ cup

SUNFLOWER BREAD

This tasty, nutty bread is great for sandwiches or toast.

	Small	Medium	Large
milk/water	2/3 cup	1 cup	1 1/3 cups
vegetable oil	1 1/2 tbs.	2 1/4 tbs.	3 tbs.
honey	1 1/2 tbs.	2 1/4 tbs.	3 tbs.
salt	1/2 tsp.	3/4 tsp.	1 tsp.
whole wheat flour	1 cup	1 1/2 cups	2 cups
bread flour	1 cup	1 1/2 cups	2 cups
yeast	1 tsp.	1 1/2 tsp.	2 tsp.

Raisin Bread Cycle   At beep add: (If National/Panasonic, add following first kneading; if Maxim or Mister Loaf, add at beginning.)

sunflower kernels	1/4 cup	1/3 cup	1/2 cup

WALNUT BREAD

This hearty loaf of bread is superb served with cheese and red wine. Walnut oil may be found in any health food store or in a well-stocked grocery store. Any vegetable oil may be substituted.

	Small	Medium	Large
water or beer	2/3 cup	1 cup	1⅓ cups
walnut oil	1 tbs.	1½ tbs.	2 tbs.
finely chopped onion	¼ cup	⅓ cup	½ cup
sugar	¾ tbs.	1 tbs.	1½ tbs.
salt	½ tsp.	¾ tsp.	1 tsp.
rosemary	⅛ tsp.	⅛ tsp.	¼ tsp.
bread flour	1 cup	1½ cups	2 cups
whole wheat flour	½ cup	¾ cup	1 cup
rye flour	½ cup	¾ cup	1 cup
yeast	1 tsp.	1½ tsp.	2½ tsp.

Raisin Bread Cycle   At beep add: (If National/Panasonic, add following first kneading; if Maxim or Mister Loaf, add at the beginning.)

	Small	Medium	Large
chopped walnuts	¼ cup	⅓ cup	½ cup

SCALLION BREAD

A great accompaniment to a barbecue meal or on a picnic.

	Small	Medium	Large
water	½ cup	¾ cup	1 cup
margarine	2 tsp.	1 tbs.	1⅓ tbs.
chopped scallion	½ cup	⅔ cup	1 cup
egg	1	1¼	2
salt	½ tsp.	⅔ tsp.	1 tsp.
sugar	½ tsp.	⅔ tsp.	1 tsp.
garlic powder	¼ tsp.	⅓ tsp.	½ tsp.
black pepper	¼ tsp.	⅓ tsp.	½ tsp.
whole wheat flour	¾ cup	1 cup	1½ cups
bread flour	1 cup	1⅔ cups	2 cups
yeast	1 tsp.	1½ tsp.	2½ tsp.
egg substitute	¼ cup	5 tbs.	½ cup

WALNUT ONION MUSHROOM BREAD

Serve this with some hot soup and a salad and you have a full meal.

	Small	Medium	Large
water	½ cup	¾ cup	1 cup
walnut oil	2 tsp.	1 tbs.	1⅓ tbs.
honey	2 tsp.	1 tbs.	1⅓ tbs.
chopped onions	2 tbs.	3 tbs.	¼ cup
sautéed sliced mushrooms	¼ cup	⅓ cup	½ cup
salt	½ tsp.	¾ tsp.	1 tsp.
whole wheat flour	½ cup	¾ cup	1 cup
bread flour	1½ cups	2¼ cups	3 cups
yeast	1 tsp.	1½ tsp.	2½ tsp.

Raisin Bread Cycle At beep add: (If National/Panasonic, add following first kneading; if Maxim or Mister Loaf, add at beginning.)

	Small	Medium	Large
chopped walnuts	2 tbs.	3 tbs.	¼ cup

Sauté mushrooms in 1 to 2 teaspoons of walnut oil until liquid is gone. If walnut oil is unavailable, any vegetable oil may be substituted.

ONION RYE

This variation on onion bread is terrific — you'll make it more than once.

	Small	Medium	Large
water	½ cup	¾ cup	1 cup
chopped onion	⅓ cup	½ cup	⅔ cup
vegetable oil	2 tsp.	1 tbs.	1⅓ tbs.
honey	2 tsp.	1 tbs.	1⅓ tbs.
salt	½ tsp.	¾ tsp.	1 tsp.
rye flour	¾ cup	1 cup	1½ cups
bread flour	1¼ cups	2 cups	2½ cups
yeast	1 tsp.	1½ tsp.	2 tsp.

ONION POPPY SEED BREAD

Even someone who does not like onions will like this bread — the poppy seed and onion combination is a true winner.

	Small	Medium	Large
water	½ cup	¾ cup	1 cup
margarine/butter	1 tbs.	1½ tbs.	2 tbs.
chopped onion	⅓ cup	½ cup	⅔ cup
salt	½ tsp.	¾ tsp.	1 tsp.
sugar	1 tsp.	1½ tsp.	2 tsp.
poppy seeds	1 tbs.	1½ tbs.	2 tbs.
whole wheat flour	1 cup	1½ cups	2 cups
bread flour	1 cup	1½ cups	2 cups
yeast	1 tsp.	1½ tsp.	2 tsp.

HERB & SPICE BREADS

PEPPER BREAD

A great accompaniment to a grilled steak dinner, and a special pick-me-up for sandwiches. You can substitute up to half the bread flour with whole wheat. Ricotta cheese may be substituted for the cottage cheese. If you desire a hotter pepper bread, you may double the amount of pepper used.

	Small	Medium	Large
milk	3 tbs.	¼ cup	6 tbs.
cottage cheese	¾ cups	1 cup	1½ cups
margarine/butter	2 tbs.	3 tbs.	4 tbs.
eggs	¾	1	1½
sugar	¾ tbs.	1 tbs.	1½ tbs.
salt	¾ tsp.	1 tsp.	1½ tsp.
coarsely ground black pepper	½ tsp.	⅔ tsp.	1 tsp.
dried chives	¾ tsp.	1 tsp.	1½ tsp.
bread flour	1½ cups	2 cups	3 cups
yeast	1 tsp.	1½ tsp.	2½ tsp.
egg substitute	3 tbs.	¼ cup	6 tbs.

HONEY CURRY BREAD

Great with chicken at dinner or on a picnic.

	Small	Medium	Large
milk/water	3⁄4 cup	1 1⁄8 cups	1 1⁄2 cups
vegetable oil	2 tsp.	1 tbs.	1 1⁄3 tbs.
honey	1 tbs.	1 1⁄2 tbs.	2 tbs.
salt	1⁄2 tsp.	3⁄4 tsp.	1 tsp.
curry powder	1 tsp.	1 1⁄2 tsp.	2 tsp.
whole wheat flour	1 cup	1 1⁄2 cups	2 cups
bread flour	1 cup	1 1⁄2 cups	2 cups
yeast	1 tsp.	1 1⁄2 tsp.	2 tsp.

OATMEAL GINGER BREAD

A tasty, low rising loaf — try it with chicken salad for brunch.

	Small	Medium	Large
water	2/3 cup	1 cup	1 1/3 cups
vegetable oil	1 tbs.	1 1/2 tbs.	2 tbs.
molasses	2 tbs.	3 tbs.	1/4 cup
salt	1/2 tsp.	3/4 tsp.	1 tsp.
ground ginger	1/2 tsp.	3/4 tsp.	1 tsp.
oats	1 cup	1 1/2 cups	2 cups
bread flour	1 cup	1 1/2 cups	2 cups
yeast	1 tsp.	1 1/2 tsp.	2 tsp.

SAFFRON BREAD

Saffron is one of the world's most expensive spices, but only a little bit is used to achieve this wonderful, tasty bread. Equally delicious without the raisins.

	Small	Medium	Large
milk	½ cup	⅔ cup	1 cup
margarine/butter	2 tbs.	2½ tbs.	3 tbs.
eggs	½	⅔	¾
salt	⅓ tsp.	½ tsp.	⅔ tsp.
sugar	2 tbs.	2½ tbs.	3 tbs.
nutmeg	¼ tsp.	⅓ tsp.	½ tsp.
powdered saffron	1/16 tsp.	1/16 tsp.	⅛ tsp.
bread flour	1½ cups	2 cups	3 cups
yeast	1 tsp.	1½ tsp.	2 tsp.

Raisin Bread Cycle   At beep add: (If National/Panasonic, add following first kneading; if Maxim or Mister Loaf, add at beginning.)

	Small	Medium	Large
currants or raisins	¼ cup	⅓ cup	½ cup
egg substitute	2 tbs.	2½ tbs.	3 tbs.

BASIL PARMESAN BREAD

This is out of this world. A must with an Italian meal. While the pre-grated Parmesan cheese may be used in this recipe, freshly grated Parmesan cheese is much better.

	Small	Medium	Large
water	¾ cup	1⅛ cups	1½ cups
olive oil	1 tbs.	1½ tbs.	2 tbs.
grated Swiss cheese	¼ cup	⅓ cup	½ cup
grated Parmesan cheese	¼ cup	⅓ cup	½ cup
salt	¼ tsp.	⅓ tsp.	½ tsp.
sugar	2 tsp.	1 tbs.	1⅓ tbs.
basil	2 tsp.	1 tbs.	1⅓ tbs.
whole wheat flour	1 cup	1½ cups	2 cups
bread flour	1 cup	1½ cups	2 cups
yeast	1 tsp.	1½ tsp.	2½ tsp.

PIZZA BREAD

A great snack bread to enjoy while watching football.

	Small	Medium	Large
pizza sauce	¾ cup	1⅛ cups	1½ cups
grated mozzarella cheese	⅓ cup	½ cup	⅔ cup
olive oil	1½ tbs.	2¼ tbs.	3 tbs.
salt	⅓ tsp.	½ tsp.	⅔ tsp.
oregano	½ tsp.	¾ tsp.	1 tsp.
whole wheat flour	1 cup	1½ cups	2 cups
bread flour	1 cup	1½ cups	2 cups
yeast	1 tsp.	1½ tsp.	2 tsp.

Raisin Bread Cycle At beep add one or two of the following: (If National/Panasonic, add following first kneading; if Maxim or Mister Loaf, add at beginning.)

	Small	Medium	Large
diced pepperoni	⅓ cup	½ cup	⅔ cup
diced mushrooms	⅓ cup	½ cup	⅔ cup
diced dried tomatoes	2 tbs.	3 tbs.	¼ cup

PEPPERONI BREAD

This is a true winner. Serve as a snack with some beer or take along on a picnic. A "must try."

	Small	Medium	Large
water	⅔ cup	1 cup	1⅓ cups
olive oil	1 tbs.	1½ tbs.	2 tbs.
salt	¼ tsp.	⅓ tsp.	½ tsp.
sugar	½ tsp.	⅔ tsp.	1 tsp.
oregano	¾ tsp.	1¼ tsp.	1½ tsp.
garlic powder	¼ tsp.	⅓ tsp.	½ tsp.
basil	¼ tsp.	⅓ tsp.	½ tsp.
whole wheat flour	⅔ cup	1 cup	1⅓ cups
bread flour	1⅓ cups	2 cups	2⅔ cups
yeast	1 tsp.	1½ tsp.	2½ tsp.

Raisin Bread Cycle   At beep add: (If National/Panasonic, add following first kneading; if Maxim or Mister Loaf, add at beginning.)

diced pepperoni	½ cup	¾ cup	1 cup

VARIATION: PEPPERONI JALAPEÑO BREAD

This bread was the result of a suggestion by USNA Midshipman Arnold and is an absolute winner. Anyone who likes spicy food will love this one.

Add to **Pepperoni Bread** at the beep: (If National/Panasonic add following the first kneading; if Maxim, add at beginning.)

grated jalapeño cheese	⅓ cup	½ cup	⅔ cup
diced jalapeño pepper	1	1½	2

MINTED HERB BREAD

*This is an absolutely superb bread. Try it! You can vary this bread by substituting up to half of the bread flour with whole wheat flour. Don't forget to triple amount of herbs if you use fresh (see page 8, **Questions and Answers**).*

	Small	Medium	Large
water	⅔ cup	1 cup	1⅓ cups
olive oil	2 tbs.	3 tbs.	¼ cup
salt	½ tsp.	⅔ tsp.	1 tsp.
sugar	½ tsp.	⅔ tsp.	1 tsp.
grated Parmesan cheese	2 tbs.	3 tbs.	¼ cup
basil	1 tsp.	1½ tsp.	2 tsp.
parsley	1 tsp.	1½ tsp.	2 tsp.
mint	1 tsp.	1½ tsp.	2 tsp.
bread flour	1½ cups	2 cups	3 cups
yeast	1 tsp.	1½ tsp.	2½ tsp.

INTERNATIONAL & HOLIDAY BREADS

EASTER BREAD

Thanks to Marcia Germaine for sharing her grandmother's recipe.

	Small	Medium	Large
milk	1/4 cup	1/3 cup	1/2 cup
water	1/4 cup	1/3 cup	1/2 cup
eggs	1	1 1/2	2
margarine/butter	4 tbs.	6 tbs.	8 tbs.
salt	1/4 tsp.	1/3 tsp.	1/2 tsp.
sugar	1/4 cup	1/3 cup	1/2 cup
anise seed	1/2 tsp.	3/4 tsp.	1 tsp.
bread flour	1 3/4 cups	2 2/3 cups	3 1/2 cups
yeast	1 tsp.	1 1/2 tsp.	2 tsp.

Raisin Bread Cycle   At beep add: (If National/Panasonic, add following first kneading; if Maxim or Mister Loaf, add at beginning.)

anise seed	1/2 tsp.	3/4 tsp.	1 tsp.

Welbilt ABM 100, DAK and Mister Loaf - use *Sweet Bread Cycle.*

egg substitute	1/4 cup	6 tbs.	1/2 cup

GREEK KOULOURA BREAD

Traditionally, this loaf is twisted and has a topping of sesame seeds. A great breakfast or brunch bread. If desired, open the machine briefly during the second rising and sprinkle sesame seeds on the top of the dough. Be careful not to spill any into the machine itself.

	Small	Medium	Large
milk	¾ cup	1 cup	1¼ cups
vegetable oil	¾ tbs.	1 tbs.	1¼ tbs.
eggs	¼	⅓	½
salt	⅓ tsp.	½ tsp.	⅔ tsp.
sugar	¾ tbs.	1 tbs.	1¼ tbs.
bread flour	1¾ cups	2⅓ cups	3½ cups
yeast	1 tsp.	1½ tsp.	2½ tsp.
egg substitute	1 tbs.	1½ tbs.	2 tbs.

ST. BASIL'S BREAD

This traditional Greek bread is usually served with one coin hidden inside which bestows luck upon the finder. I do not recommend including it in the bread as you may damage your machine! (You may use a single raisin added at the beep, if desired.) St. Basil's bread is a delicious, sweet bread which disappears quickly.

	Small	**Medium**	**Large**
milk	1/3 cup+1 tbs.	1/2 cup	3/4 cup
margarine/butter	2 tbs.	2½ tbs.	4 tbs.
egg	1	1¼	2
sugar	¼ cup	⅓ cup	½ cup
salt	¼ tsp.	⅓ tsp.	½ tsp.
grated lemon peel	¼ tsp.	⅓ tsp.	½ tsp.
cinnamon	⅛ tsp.	⅛ tsp.	¼ tsp.
nutmeg	¼ tsp.	⅓ tsp.	½ tsp.
ground cloves	1/16 tsp.	1/16 tsp.	⅛ tsp.
bread flour	1½ cups	2 cups	3 cups
yeast	1 tsp.	1½ tsp.	2 tsp.

GREEK SUNDAY BREAD

Another wonderful Greek bread! If desired, open the machine during the second rising and place sesame seeds on top of the dough.

	Small	Medium	Large
milk	5⁄8 cup	1 cup-1½ tbs.	1¼ cups
margarine/butter	2 tbs.	3 tbs.	4 tbs.
eggs	¾	1	1½
salt	½ tsp.	¾ tsp.	1 tsp.
sugar	1½ tbs.	2⅓ tbs.	3 tbs.
cinnamon	1⁄8 tsp.	1⁄8 tsp.	¼ tsp.
anise	1⁄8 tsp.	1⁄8 tsp.	¼ tsp.
grated orange peel	1⁄8 tsp.	1⁄8 tsp.	¼ tsp.
allspice	1⁄16 tsp.	1⁄16 tsp.	1⁄8 tsp.
bread flour	1¾ cups	2⅓ cups	3½ cups
yeast	1 tsp.	1 tsp.	2 tsp.

Welbilt ABM 100, DAK and Mister Loaf - use *Sweet Bread Cycle.*

egg substitute	3 tbs.	¼ cup	6 tbs.

GREEK EASTER BREAD (LAMBROPSOMO)

A wonderful, sweet bread which is good any time of the year.

	Small	Medium	Large
milk	5⁄8 cup	1 cup-1½ tbs.	1¼ cups
margarine/butter	2 tbs.	3 tbs.	4 tbs.
eggs	3⁄4	1	1½
salt	3⁄4 tsp.	1⅛ tsp.	1½ tsp.
sugar	¼ cup	⅓ cup	½ cup
cinnamon	⅛ tsp.	⅛ tsp.	¼ tsp.
anise	⅛ tsp.	⅛ tsp.	¼ tsp.
grated orange peel	⅛ tsp.	⅛ tsp.	¼ tsp.
allspice	1⁄16 tsp.	1⁄16 tsp.	⅛ tsp.
bread flour	1¾ cups	2⅓ cups	3½ cups
yeast	1 tsp.	1½ tsp.	2 tsp.

Welbilt ABM 100, DAK and Mister Loaf - use *Sweet Bread Cycle*

| egg substitute | 3 tbs. | ¼ cup | 6 tbs. |

PORTUGUESE EASTER BREAD

*My daughter, Rachel, refused to let me give any of this bread away to tasters —
she loves it for sandwiches!*

	Small	**Medium**	**Large**
milk	½ cup	⅔ cup	1 cup
eggs	1	1½	2
margarine/butter	1 tbs.	1¼ tbs.	2 tbs.
sugar	¼ cup	⅓ cup	½ cup
salt	½ tsp.	⅔ tsp.	1 tsp.
bread flour	1½ cups	2 cups	3 cups
yeast	1 tsp.	1½ tsp.	2 tsp.

Welbilt ABM 100, DAK and Mister Loaf - use *Sweet Bread Cycle.*

egg substitute	¼ cup	6 tbs.	½ cup

PORTUGUESE BROA (CORN BREAD)

This Portuguese cornmeal bread is outstanding. The white cornmeal makes this a very distinctive, delicious loaf. Most recipes for Broa stipulate using white cornmeal; yellow or blue may also be used as a variation.

	Small	Medium	Large
water	2/3 cup	1 cup	1 1/3 cups
olive oil	1 1/3 tbs.	2 tbs.	2 2/3 tbs.
salt	1/2 tsp.	3/4 tsp.	1 tsp.
sugar	1/2 tsp.	3/4 tsp.	1 tsp.
white cornmeal	2/3 cup	1 cup	1 1/3 cups
bread flour	1 1/3 cups	2 cups	2 2/3 cups
yeast	1 tsp.	1 1/2 tsp.	2 1/2 tsp.

FRENCH PEAR BREAD

This is well worth the time involved to make the pear puree. Fresh pears should be boiled in water until soft; canned pears should be rinsed. Puree in blender or food processor. Pepper may be omitted for a different taste, and dried pears, found in some grocery stores or health food stores, may be added for another variation.

	Small	Medium	Large
pear puree	1/2 cup	3/4 cup	1 cup
vegetable oil	1 tbs.	1 1/2 tbs.	2 tbs.
honey	1 tbs.	1 1/2 tbs.	2 tbs.
eggs	1	1 1/2	2
salt	1/3 tsp.	1/2 tsp.	2/3 tsp.
coarsely ground black pepper	1/8 tsp.	1/8 tsp.	1/4 tsp.
bread flour	1 1/2 cups	2 1/4 cups	3 cups
yeast	1 tsp.	1 1/2 tsp.	2 1/2 tsp.

Raisin Bread Cycle Optional — at the beep: (If National/Panasonic, add following the first kneading; Maxim or Mister Loaf, add at the beginning.)

	Small	Medium	Large
diced, dried pears	1/4 cup	1/3 cup	1/2 cup
egg substitute	1/4 cup	6 tbs.	1/2 cup

GERMAN EASTER BREAD

This bread is traditionally formed into a braided circle and served with dyed Easter eggs placed in the center. Here is a wonderful "lazy" way to make it.

	Small	Medium	Large
milk	1/3 cup	1/2 cup	2/3 cup
margarine/butter	4 tbs.	6 tbs.	8 tbs.
eggs	1	1 1/2	2
almond extract	1/2 tsp.	3/4 tsp.	1 tsp.
salt	1/4 tsp.	1/3 tsp.	1/2 tsp.
sugar	2 tbs.	3 tbs.	1/4 cup
grated lemon peel	1/4 tsp.	1/3 tsp.	1/2 tsp.
anise	1/4 tsp.	1/3 tsp.	1/2 tsp.
bread flour	1 1/2 cups	2 1/4 cups	3 cups
yeast	1 tsp.	1 1/2 tsp.	2 1/2 tsp.

Raisin Bread Cycle   At beep add: (If National/Panasonic, add following first kneading; if Maxim or Mister Loaf, add at beginning.)

golden raisins	1/4 cup	1/3 cup	1/2 cup
sliced almonds	2 tbs.	3 tbs.	1/4 cup
egg substitute	1/4 cup	6 tbs.	1/2 cup

ITALIAN EASTER BREAD

This rich, cheesy bread is not as sweet as many of the other Easter breads.

	Small	Medium	Large
milk	½ cup	¾ cup	1 cup
olive oil	1½ tbs.	2¼ tbs.	3 tbs.
margarine/butter	4 tbs.	6 tbs.	8 tbs.
eggs	1	1½	2
salt	¼ tsp.	⅓ tsp.	½ tsp.
sugar	½ tsp.	¾ tsp.	1 tsp.
grated Parmesan cheese	½ cup	¾ cup	1 cup
black pepper	⅛ tsp.	⅛ tsp.	¼ tsp.
bread flour	1½ cups	2¼ cups	3 cups
yeast	1 tsp.	1½ tsp.	2½ tsp.

Welbilt ABM 100, DAK and Mister Loaf - use *Sweet Bread Cycle.*

| egg substitute | ¼ cup | 6 tbs. | ½ cup |

ITALIAN SPRING BREAD

Anise imparts an exotic taste to this bread.

	Small	Medium	Large
water	½ cup	¾ cup	1 cup
vegetable oil	1 tbs.	1½ tbs.	2 tbs.
honey	1 tsp.	1½ tsp.	2 tsp.
salt	⅓ tsp.	½ tsp.	⅔ tsp.
anise	2 tbs.	3 tbs.	¼ cup
bread flour	1½ cups	2¼ cups	3 cups
yeast	1 tsp.	1½ tsp.	2½ tsp.

Raisin Bread Cycle   At beep add: (If National/Panasonic, add following first kneading; if Maxim or Mister Loaf, add at beginning.)

golden raisins	⅓ cup	½ cup	⅔ cup

ENGLISH GOOD FRIDAY BREAD

Most people equate caraway seeds with rye — that is, until they try this bread!

	Small	Medium	Large
water	½ cup	¾ cup	1 cup
margarine/butter	2 tbs.	3 tbs.	4 tbs.
salt	½ tsp.	⅔ tsp.	1 tsp.
sugar	2 tsp.	1 tbs.	1⅓ tbs.
caraway seeds	⅔ tsp.	1 tsp.	1⅓ tsp.
bread flour	1½ cups	2 cups	3 cups
yeast	1 tsp.	1½ tsp.	2½ tsp.

ENGLISH NEW YEAR'S RUM BREAD

This traditional bread is served at New Year's with a coin hidden inside to bestow luck on the finder. Do not attempt to do that in your machine, though. If you wish, you may use a single raisin.

	Small	Medium	Large
water	1/3 cup+1 tbs.	1/2 cup	3/4 cup
light rum	2 tsp.	1 tbs.	1 1/2 tbs.
margarine/butter	1/2 tbs.	2 tbs.	3 tbs.
sugar	1/4 cup	1/3 cup	1/2 cup
salt	1/2 tsp.	2/3 tsp.	1 tsp.
bread flour	1 1/2 cups	2 cups	3 cups
yeast	1 tsp.	1 1/2 tsp.	2 1/2 tsp.

Welbilt ABM 100, DAK and Mister Loaf - use *Sweet Bread Cycle.*

WELSH YEAST CAKE (BARA BRITH)

This is a rich cake-like bread — a real treat.

	Small	Medium	Large
milk	½ cup	¾ cup	1 cup
margarine/butter	4 tbs.	6 tbs.	8 tbs.
molasses	1½ tsp.	2 tsp.	1 tbs.
egg	½	¾	1
salt	½ tsp.	⅔ tsp.	1 tsp.
sugar	2 tbs.	3 tbs.	¼ cup
caraway seeds	½ tsp.	¾ tsp.	1 tsp.
bread flour	1¾ cups	2⅔ cups	3½ cups
yeast	1 tsp.	1½ tsp.	2 tsp.

Raisin Bread Cycle At beep add: (If National/Panasonic, add following first kneading; if Maxim or Mister Loaf, add at beginning.)

raisins	¼ cup	⅓ cup	½ cup
nuts	¼ cup	⅓ cup	½ cup

Welbilt ABM 100, DAK and Mister Loaf - use *Sweet Bread Cycle.*

egg substitute	2 tbs.	3 tbs.	¼ cup

SWEDISH JULBROD (CHRISTMAS BREAD)

The cardamom imparts a distinctive, delicious taste.

	Small	Medium	Large
milk	½ cup	¾ cup	1 cup
margarine/butter	2 tbs.	3 tbs.	4 tbs.
egg	½	¾	1
sugar	2 tbs.	3 tbs.	¼ cup
salt	½ tsp.	⅔ tsp.	1 tsp.
cardamom	½ tsp.	⅔ tsp.	1 tsp.
bread flour	1½ cups	2¼ cups	3 cups
yeast	1 tsp.	1½ tsp.	2½ tsp.

Raisin Bread Cycle   At beep add: (If National/Panasonic, add following first kneading; if Maxim or Mister Loaf, add at beginning.)

	Small	Medium	Large
raisins	⅓ cup	½ cup	⅔ cup
sliced citron	⅓ cup	½ cup	⅔ cup
chopped almonds	1 tbs.	1½ tbs.	2 tbs.

Welbilt ABM 100, DAK and Mister Loaf - use *Sweet Bread Cycle.*

	Small	Medium	Large
egg substitute	2 tbs.	3 tbs.	¼ cup

SWEDISH CHOCOLATE BREAD

Traditionally this bread is made as a chocolate-filled coffee bread. This is a variation devised for ease in the machines. Use hazelnuts or walnuts.

	Small	Medium	Large
milk	1/3 cup+ 1 tbs.	1/2 cup	3/4 cup
margarine/butter	1 1/2 tbs.	2 tbs.	3 tbs.
eggs	3/4	1	1 1/2
sugar	2 1/2 tbs.	1/4 cup	1/3 cup
salt	1/3 tsp.	1/2 tsp.	3/4 tsp.
unsweetened cocoa	2 tsp.	1 tbs.	1 1/2 tbs.
cinnamon	1/16 tsp.	1/8 tsp.	1/8 tsp.
bread flour	1 1/2 cups	2 cups	3 cups
yeast	1 tsp.	1 tsp.	1 1/2 tsp.

Raisin Bread Cycle At beep add: (If National/Panasonic, add following first kneading; if Maxim or Mister Loaf, add at beginning.)

chopped hazelnuts	3 tbs.	1/4 cup	1/3 cup

Welbilt ABM 100, DAK or Mister Loaf - use *Sweet Bread Cycle.*

egg substitute	3 tbs.	1/4 cup	6 tbs.

SCANDINAVIAN RYE

This is similar to a Swedish "Limpa." The fennel gives it a wonderful, uplifting taste.

	Small	Medium	Large
water or milk	2/3 cup	1 cup	1⅓ cups
vegetable oil	1½ tbs.	2¼ tbs.	3 tbs.
molasses	1½ tbs.	2¼ tbs.	3 tbs.
salt	½ tsp.	¾ tsp.	1 tsp.
baking soda	⅛ tsp.	⅛ tsp.	¼ tsp.
fennel seeds	¾ tsp.	1 tsp.	1½ tsp.
caraway seeds	¾ tsp.	1 tsp.	1½ tsp.
grated orange peel	¾ tsp.	1 tsp.	1½ tsp.
rye flour	1 cup	1½ cups	2 cups
bread flour	1 cup	1½ cups	2 cups
yeast	1½ tsp.	2 tsp.	2½ tsp.

FINNISH EASTER BREAD

Rye flour makes this a unique Easter Bread.

	Small	Medium	Large
light cream or milk	⅔ cup	1 cup	1⅓ cups
margarine/butter	2 tbs.	3 tbs.	4 tbs.
eggs	1	1½	2
salt	⅓ tsp.	½ tsp.	⅔ tsp.
sugar	2 tbs.	3 tbs.	¼ cup
ground cardamom	½ tsp.	¾ tsp.	1 tsp.
lemon peel	½ tsp.	¾ tsp.	1 tsp.
orange peel	½ tsp.	¾ tsp.	1 tsp.
rye flour	½ cup	¾ cup	1 cup
bread flour	1½ cups	2¼ cups	3 cups
yeast	1 tsp.	1½ tsp.	2½ tsp.

Raisin Bread Cycle At beep add: (If National/Panasonic, add following first kneading; if Maxim or Mister Loaf, add at the beginning.)

	Small	Medium	Large
golden raisins	¼ cup	⅓ cup	½ cup
chopped almonds	¼ cup	⅓ cup	½ cup

Welbilt ABM 100, DAK and Mister Loaf - use *Sweet Bread Cycle.*

	Small	Medium	Large
egg substitute	¼ cup	6 tbs.	½ cup

FINNISH PULLA

Cardamom is common in Scandinavian breads and gives a sweet flavoring.

	Small	**Medium**	**Large**
milk	1/3 cup	1/2 cup	2/3 cup
eggs	3/4	1	1 1/2
margarine/butter	3 tbs.	4 1/2 tbs.	6 tbs.
sugar	2 3/4 tbs.	1/4 cup	5 1/2 tbs.
salt	1/2 tsp.	3/4 tsp.	1 tsp.
crushed cardamom	1/2 tsp.	3/4 tsp.	1 tsp.
bread flour	1 1/2 cups	2 1/4 cups	3 cups
yeast	1 tsp.	1 1/2 tsp.	2 tsp.

Raisin Bread Cycle   At beep add: (If National/Panasonic, add following the first kneading; if Maxim or Mister Loaf, add at beginning.)

raisins	1/3 cup	1/2 cup	2/3 cup

Welbilt ABM 100, DAK and Mister Loaf - use *Sweet Bread Cycle.*

egg substitute	3 tbs.	1/4 cup	6 tbs.

MOROCCAN BREAD

Semolina flour is, in this country, usually only used to make pasta. It is, however, also wonderful in bread. This bread is traditionally made as a large round, puffy loaf. Try it — you'll like it!

	Small	Medium	Large
water	⅔ cup	1 cup	1⅓ cups
olive oil	2 tbs.	3 tbs.	¼ cup
salt	⅔ tsp.	1 tsp.	1⅓ tsp.
sugar	⅔ tsp.	1 tsp.	1⅓ tsp.
anise seeds	2 tsp.	1 tbs.	1⅓ tbs.
sesame seeds	½ tsp.	¾ tsp.	1 tsp.
whole wheat flour	½ cup	¾ cup	1 cup
rye flour	½ cup	¾ cup	1 cup
semolina flour	½ cup	¾ cup	1 cup
bread flour	½ cup	¾ cup	1 cup
yeast	1 tsp.	1½ tsp.	2½ tsp.

MOROCCAN ANISE BREAD

An outstanding change-of-pace bread. The anise gives it nice flavor.

	Small	**Medium**	**Large**
milk or water	2/3 cup	1 cup	1 1/3 cups
margarine/butter	2 tbs.	3 tbs.	4 tbs.
salt	1/3 tsp.	1/2 tsp.	2/3 tsp.
sugar	2 tbs.	3 tbs.	1/4 cup
anise seed	1/2 tsp.	3/4 tsp.	1 tsp.
bread flour	1 1/2 cups	2 1/4 cups	3 cups
yeast	1 tsp.	1 1/2 tsp.	2 tsp.

ETHIOPIAN HONEY BREAD

This is an adaptation of one of our family's favorite breads from pre-machine days. You, too, will soon love this.

	Small	Medium	Large
water	½ cup	⅔ cup	1 cup
vegetable oil	1½ tbs.	2¼ tbs.	3 tbs.
honey	2 tbs.	3 tbs.	¼ cup
salt	¼ tsp.	⅓ tsp.	½ tsp.
coriander	¾ tsp.	1⅛ tsp.	1½ tsp.
cinnamon	¼ tsp.	⅓ tsp.	½ tsp.
cloves	⅛ tsp.	⅛ tsp.	¼ tsp.
bread flour	1½ cups	2¼ cups	3 cups
nonfat dry milk	2 tbs.	3 tbs.	¼ cup
yeast	1 tsp.	1½ tsp.	2 tsp.

WEST INDIES BANANA BREAD

This is an adaptation of a delicious quick bread, or non-yeast bread, from the West Indies. Vanilla extract may be substituted for coconut extract.

	Small	Medium	Large
ripe mashed bananas	5/8 cup	3/4 cup	1 1/8 cups
margarine/butter	3 tbs.	4 tbs.	6 tbs.
egg	1/2	3/4	1
coconut extract	1/2 tsp.	2/3 tsp.	1 tsp.
salt	1/3 tsp.	1/2 tsp.	3/4 tsp.
sugar	1/4 cup	1/3 cup	1/2 cup
cinnamon	1/4 tsp.	1/3 tsp.	1/2 tsp.
nutmeg	1/8 tsp.	1/8 tsp.	1/8 tsp.
shredded coconut	1 tbs.	1 1/3 tbs.	2 tbs.
bread flour	1 1/2 cups	2 cups	3 cups
yeast	1 tsp.	1 tsp.	1 1/2 tsp.

Raisin Bread Cycle   At beep add: (If National/Panasonic, add following first kneading; if Maxim or Mister Loaf, add at beginning.)

raisins	1/4 cup	1/3 cup	1/2 cup

Welbilt ABM 100, DAK and Mister Loaf - use *Sweet Bread Cycle.*

egg substitute	2 tbs.	3 tbs.	1/4 cup

MEXICAN SWEET BREAD

This wonderful sweet bread is often used for sandwiches in this household full of kids.

	Small	Medium	Large
milk	½ cup	¾ cup	1 cup
margarine/butter	2 tbs.	3 tbs.	4 tbs.
eggs	1	1½	2
salt	½ tsp.	¾ tsp.	1 tsp.
sugar	2 tbs.	3 tbs.	¼ cup
bread flour	1½ cups	2¼ cups	3 cups
yeast	1 tsp.	1½ tsp.	2 tsp.

Welbilt ABM 100, DAK and Mister Loaf - Use *Sweet Bread Cycle.*

egg substitute	¼ cup	6 tbs.	½ cup

MEXICAN KING'S BREAD

Absolutely delicious. The rum adds a subtle yet distinctive taste. This bread is traditionally served on the twelfth day of Christmas to mark the arrival of the three kings in Bethlehem. A small porcelain doll is hidden inside and whoever receives the doll must give a party during the holiday season.

	Small	Medium	Large
milk	1/3 cup	1/2 cup	2/3 cup
margarine/butter	2 tbs.	2 1/2 tbs.	4 tbs.
light rum	1 1/2 tsp.	2 tsp.	1 tbs.
egg	1	1 1/4	2
sugar	2 tbs.	2 1/2 tbs.	1/4 cup
salt	1/2 tsp.	2/3 tsp.	1 tsp.
grated orange peel	1/2 tsp.	2/3 tsp.	1 tsp.
bread flour	1 1/2 cups	2 cups	3 cups
yeast	1 tsp.	1 1/2 tsp.	2 tsp.

Welbilt ABM 100, DAK and Mister Loaf - use *Sweet Bread Cycle.*

egg substitute	1/4 cup	5 tbs.	1/2 cup

MEXICAN CHRISTMAS BREAD

The candied cherries give this a wonderful color and flavor.

	Small	Medium	Large
milk	⅓ cup+1 tbs.	½ cup	¾ cup
margarine/butter	¾ tbs.	1 tbs.	1½ tbs.
eggs	¾	1	1½
salt	¼ tsp.	⅓ tsp.	½ tsp.
sugar	1 tbs.+1 tsp.	1½ tbs.	2 tbs.
orange peel	1⅛ tsp.	¼ tsp.	⅓ tsp.
bread flour	1½ cups	2 cups	3 cups
yeast	1 tsp.	1 tsp.	1½ tsp.

Raisin Bread Cycle At beep add: (If National/Panasonic, add following first kneading; if Maxim or Mister Loaf, add at beginning.)

chopped candied cherries	¼ cup	⅓ cup	½ cup
chopped walnuts	1½ tbs.	2 tbs.	3 tbs.

Welbilt ABM 100, DAK and Mister Loaf - use *Sweet Bread Cycle*.

egg substitute	2 tbs.	¼ cup	6 tbs.

BREAD OF THE DEAD (PAN DE MUERTOS)

This is the bread carried to and eaten at the graves of relatives on All Souls Day. Traditionally, it is round and decorated with "bones" made from the dough. This is almost like eating a cake instead of bread — not one of your more dietetic!

	Small	Medium	Large
water	1/4 cup	1/3 cup	1/2 cup
margarine/butter	3 tbs.	4 1/2 tbs.	6 tbs.
eggs	3	4 1/2	6
sugar	1/4 cup	3/8 cup	1/2 cup
salt	1/2 tsp.	3/4 tsp.	1 tsp.
grated orange peel	1/4 tsp.	1/3 tsp.	1/2 tsp.
anise	1/8 tsp.	1/8 tsp.	1/4 tsp.
bread flour	1 3/4 cups	2 1/3 cups	3 1/2 cups
yeast	1 tsp.	1 1/2 tsp.	2 1/2 tsp.

Welbilt ABM 100, DAK and Mister Loaf - use *Sweet Bread Cycle*.

egg substitute	3/4 cup	1 1/8 cups	1 1/2 cups

BRAZILIAN EASTER BREAD

The Brazil nuts give this a wonderful, distinctive flavor. A favorite.

	Small	Medium	Large
milk	½ cup	¾ cup	1 cup
margarine/butter	2 tbs.	3 tbs.	4 tbs.
eggs	½	¾	1
salt	⅓ tsp.	½ tsp.	⅔ tsp.
sugar	1½ tbs.	2¼ tbs.	3 tbs.
cinnamon	¼ tsp.	⅓ tsp.	½ tsp.
nutmeg	⅛ tsp.	⅛ tsp.	¼ tsp.
allspice	⅛ tsp.	⅛ tsp.	¼ tsp.
bread flour	1½ cups	2¼ cups	3 cups
yeast	1 tsp.	1½ tsp.	2 tsp.

Raisin Bread Cycle   At beep add: (If National/Panasonic, add following first kneading; if Maxim or Mister Loaf, add at beginning.)

	Small	Medium	Large
golden raisins	2 tbs.	3 tbs.	¼ cup
dried apricots	2 tbs.	3 tbs.	¼ cup
chopped Brazil nuts	2 tbs.	3 tbs.	¼ cup

Welbilt ABM 100, DAK and Mister Loaf - use *Sweet Bread Cycle*.

	Small	Medium	Large
egg substitute	2 tbs.	3 tbs.	¼ cup

RUSSIAN EASTER BREAD (KULICH)

Outstanding. Pick your choice of any two or three of the fruits. Soak raisins in the sherry or amaretto for at least 15 minutes.

	Small	Medium	Large
milk	½ cup	¾ cup	1 cup
margarine/butter	1 tbs.	1½ tbs.	2 tbs.
eggs	1	1½	2
salt	⅓ tsp.	½ tsp.	⅔ tsp.
sugar	¼ cup	⅓ cup	½ cup
grated lemon peel	⅔ tsp.	1 tsp.	1⅓ tsp.
bread flour	1¾ cups	2⅔ cups	3½ cups
yeast	1 tsp.	1½ tsp.	2 tsp.

Raisin Bread Cycle At beep add: (If National/Panasonic, add following first kneading; if Maxim or Mister Loaf, add at beginning.)

	Small	Medium	Large
sherry or amaretto	1 tbs.	1½ tbs.	2 tbs.
golden raisins	2 tbs.	3 tbs.	¼ cup
dark raisins	2 tbs.	3 tbs.	¼ cup
candied cherries	2 tbs.	3 tbs.	¼ cup
candied pineapple	2 tbs.	3 tbs.	¼ cup
chopped almonds	2 tbs.	3 tbs.	¼ cup

RUSSIAN KRENDL

Traditionally this is made as a filled, coffee-cake type bread.

	Small	**Medium**	**Large**
milk	⅜ cup	½ cup	¾ cup
margarine/butter	1 tbs.	1½ tbs.	2 tbs.
vanilla extract	½ tsp.	¾ tsp.	1 tsp.
eggs	1	1½	2
salt	½ tsp.	¾ tsp.	1 tsp.
sugar	1 tbs.	1½ tbs.	2 tbs.
bread flour	1½ cups	2¼ cups	3 cups
yeast	1 tsp.	1½ tsp.	2 tsp.

Raisin Bread Cycle At beep add: (If National/Panasonic, add following first kneading; if Maxim or Mister Loaf, add at beginning.)

sautéed diced apple	¾ cup	1⅛ cup	1½ cups
diced prunes, optional	2 tbs.	3 tbs.	¼ cup
diced apricots, optional	2 tbs.	3 tbs.	¼ cup

Sauté apples in 1, 1½, 2 tbs. each of margarine/butter and sugar until just soft. Drain excess liquid; cool to room temperature prior to adding to dough.

Welbilt ABM 100, DAK and Mister Loaf - *use Sweet Bread Cycle.*

egg substitute	¼ cup	6 tbs.	½ cup

UKRAINIAN BLACK BREAD

This is a very moist bread. The consistency reminds me of an English muffin or peasant bread.

	Small	Medium	Large
strong coffee	1 cup-1½ tbs.	1¼ cups	1⅔ cups
molasses	⅔ tsp.	1 tsp.	1⅓ tsp.
salt	⅓ tsp.	½ tsp.	⅔ tsp.
rye flour	1⅓ cups	2 cups	2⅔ cups
bread flour	⅔ cups	1 cup	1⅓ cups
yeast	1 tsp.	1½ tsp.	2½ tsp.

Note: You may wish to use a whole grain setting (Maxim, National/Panasonic 100% Whole Wheat, or Zojirushi programmable) if available. This also tested well on regular white cycles.

VIENNESE EASTER BREAD

Here is a bread with a delectable, light airy form.

	Small	Medium	Large
milk	½ cup	⅔ cup	1 cup
rum	1 tbs.	1½ tbs.	2 tbs.
eggs	1	1½	2
margarine/butter	2 tbs.	3 tbs.	4 tbs.
salt	⅓ tsp.	½ tsp.	⅔ tsp.
sugar	2 tbs.	3 tbs.	¼ cup
bread flour	1½ cups	2¼ cups	3 cups
yeast	1 tsp.	1½ tsp.	2 tsp.

Raisin Bread Cycle   At beep add: (If National/Panasonic, add following first kneading; if Maxim or Mister Loaf, add at beginning.)

	Small	Medium	Large
golden raisins	1 tbs.	1½ tbs.	2 tbs.
chopped citron	1 tbs.	1½ tbs.	2 tbs.
slivered almonds	1 tbs.	1½ tbs.	2 tbs.

Welbilt ABM 100, DAK and Mister Loaf - use *Sweet Bread Cycle*.

	Small	Medium	Large
egg substitute	¼ cup	6 tbs.	½ cup

VIENNA BREAD

You'll enjoy this flavorful bread. The dough would make superb dinner rolls too, I am sure.

	Small	**Medium**	**Large**
water	5⁄8 cup	1 cup-1½ tbs.	1¼ cups
vegetable oil	1½ tsp.	2 tsp.	1 tbs.
sugar	3⁄4 tsp.	1 tsp.	1½ tsp.
salt	3⁄4 tsp.	1 tsp.	1½ tsp.
bread flour	1½ cups	2 cups	3 cups
nonfat dry milk	1½ tbs.	2 tbs.	3 tbs.
yeast	1 tsp.	1½ tsp.	2½ tsp.

COFFEE BREADS

All breads in this chapter are made on the dough cycle, removed and shaped according to one of the following directions:

JELLY-ROLL - Remove dough from machine and roll into a rectangle. Spread filling evenly on top. Roll in a jelly-roll fashion starting at the wide end. Pinch seams closed. Place on a greased baking sheet, cover and let rise about 30-45 minutes (if not otherwise specified).

MONKEY BREADS - Remove dough from machine and separate into as many 1-1½-inch balls as you can. Roll the balls in the melted butter and then the coating. Place the balls into a loaf pan, tube pan or holiday-shaped pan (such as a heart-shaped pan for Valentine's Day), cover and let rise for approximately one hour. Bake in a preheated 350° oven for 30 to 40 minutes or until golden brown.

WREATH - remove dough from machine. If there is a filling, first jelly-roll (above). If there is no filling, roll the dough into a rope shape. Take the rope shape and form it into a circle, pinching the seam closed. With scissors, cut at ⅔-inch to 1-inch intervals and turn cut sections up. Place on a greased baking sheet, cover and let rise for approximately 45 minutes. Bake in a preheated 350° oven for 30 to 40 minutes or until golden brown.

AMARETTO BREAD

This is superb for a buffet — both attractive and delicious. Great during the Christmas holidays or any other time of year. Follow directions for monkey bread or wreath, page 128.

	1 Large	**2 Small**	**2 Large**
amaretto	¼ cup	⅓ cup	½ cup
water	½ cup	¾ cup	1 cup
margarine/butter	1 tbs.	1½ tbs.	2 tbs.
egg	1	1½	2
almond extract	½ tsp.	¾ tsp.	1 tsp.
salt	⅓ tsp.	½ tsp.	⅔ tsp.
sugar	1 tbs.	1½ tbs.	2 tbs.
bread flour	2 cups	3 cups	4 cups
yeast	1 tsp.	1½ tsp.	2½ tsp.
Roll dough balls in:			
melted butter	4 tbs.	6 tbs.	8 tbs.
chopped almonds	½ cup	⅔ cup	1 cup
egg substitute	¼ cup	6 tbs.	½ cup

POPPY SEED MONKEY BREAD

*An attractive addition to any picnic or buffet. Follow directions for monkey bread or wreath, page 128. Or make **Parmesan Monkey Bread**: substitute grated Parmesan cheese for poppy seeds, and cut sugar in half.*

	Small	Medium	Large
milk or water	½ cup	¾ cup	1 cup
margarine/butter	1 tbs.	1½ tbs.	2 tbs.
almond/vanilla extract	1 tsp.	1½ tsp.	2 tsp.
egg	1	1½	2
salt	⅓ tsp.	½ tsp.	⅔ tsp.
sugar	2 tbs.	3 tbs.	¼ cup
bread flour	2 cups	3 cups	4 cups
yeast	1 tsp.	1½ tsp.	2½ tsp.
Roll dough balls in:			
melted butter	4 tbs.	6 tbs.	8 tbs.
poppy seeds	¼ cup	⅓ cup	½ cup
egg substitute	¼ cup	6 tbs.	½ cup

PUMPKIN CHEESE NUT ROLL

Festive for fall and fabulous. People will ask you for the recipe, I am sure. Either canned or fresh, cooked and mashed pumpkin may be used.

	1 Large	2 Small	2 Large
water	¼ cup	⅓ cup	½ cup
pumpkin	⅔ cup	1 cup	1⅓ cup
vegetable oil	1 tbs.	1½ tbs.	2 tbs.
honey	2 tbs.	3 tbs.	¼ cup
salt	½ tsp.	¾ tsp.	1 tsp.
cinnamon	½ tsp.	¾ tsp.	1 tsp.
allspice	¼ tsp.	⅓ tsp.	½ tsp.
nutmeg	¼ tsp.	⅓ tsp.	½ tsp.
ground cloves	⅛ tsp.	⅛ tsp.	¼ tsp.
bread flour	2 cups	3 cups	4 cups
yeast	1 tsp.	1½ tsp.	2 tsp.

Filling

softened cream cheese	4 oz.	6 oz.	8 oz.
vanilla extract	¼ tsp.	⅓ tsp.	½ tsp.
confectioners sugar	½ cup	¾ cup	1 cup
chopped walnuts/pecans	½ cup	¾ cup	1 cup

Mix ingredients together. Follow directions for jelly-roll or wreath on page 128. Bake in a preheated 350° oven for 40 minutes or until golden brown.

POLISH WALNUT AND POPPY SEED BUNS

These buns are well worth the time to prepare the filling. Better make lots—you'll need them!

	Small (9)	Medium (14)	Large (18)
milk	⅓ cup	½ cup	⅔ cup
margarine/butter	1 tbs.	2 tbs.	3 tbs.
eggs	¾	1	1½
sugar	1 tbs.	1½ tbs.	2 tbs.
salt	½ tsp.	¾ tsp.	1 tsp.
bread flour	1½ cups	2¼ cups	3 cups
yeast	1 tsp.	1½ tsp.	2 tsp.

Filling

milk	2 tbs.	¼ cup	6 tbs.
honey	1 tbs.	1½ tbs.	2 tbs.
sugar	1½ tsp.	1 tbs.	1½ tbs.
bread flour	1½ tsp.	1 tbs.	1½ tbs.
poppy seeds	1½ tbs.	2 tbs.	3 tbs.
chopped walnuts	⅔ cup	1 cup	1⅓ cups

Bring all filling ingredients to a boil over medium heat; set aside to cool. Follow directions for jelly-roll, page 128. Slice into the appropriate number of slices. Place each slice in a well-greased muffin tin, cover and let rise for about ½ hour. Bake in a preheated 375° oven for 20 to 25 minutes.

egg substitute	3 tbs.	¼ cup	6 tbs.

BREAD COOKIES

I make these all the time with my kids — so easy in the machine — and without all that sugar! Great for snacks or parties.

	Small	Medium	Large
milk/water	½ cup	¾ cup	1 cup
margarine/butter	1 tbs.	1½ tbs.	2 tbs.
sugar	1½ tbs.	2¼ tbs.	3 tbs.
salt	⅓ tsp.	½ tsp.	⅔ tsp.
bread flour	2 cups	3 cups	4 cups
yeast	1 tsp.	1½ tsp.	2 tsp.

Remove dough from machine and roll to ¼-inch thickness. Cut shapes with cookie cutters and place on a greased baking sheet. Let rise for 10 to 15 minutes, and then bake in a preheated 375° oven for 10 to 15 minutes. If desired, you may turn the "cookies" over once during the baking to achieve a golden brown appearance on both sides. The "cookies" will puff during baking.

FRENCH CHOCOLATE BUNS

A chocolate-lover's dream come true.

	Small (8)	Medium (12)	Large (16)
milk	½ cup	¾ cup	1 cup
margarine/butter	2 tbs.	3 tbs.	4 tbs.
eggs	1	1½	2
vanilla	¾ tsp.	1⅛ tsp.	1½ tsp.
sugar	1 tbs.	1½ tbs.	2 tbs.
salt	¼ tsp.	⅓ tsp.	½ tsp.
bread flour	2 cups	3 cups	4 cups
yeast	1 tsp.	1½ tsp.	2 tsp.

For filling, use semi-sweet milk chocolate morsels or chips, or use a candy bar or two broken into pieces.

Roll dough into a large rectangle of approximately ¼" in thickness. With a pastry wheel or knife, cut into the corresponding number of squares. Place several chips (I use about 1 tbs.) onto the dough and fold the dough over so that the chocolate is encased. Place the buns on a buttered baking sheet and bake in a preheated 350° oven for 20 to 25 minutes.

egg substitute	¼ cup	6 tbs.	½ cup

CINNAMON SWIRL

This was developed with my brother-in-law, Larry, to recreate one of his childhood favorites. It will soon become one of your favorites too!

	Small (1)	Medium (1)	Large (2)
water	5⁄8 cup	3⁄4 cup	1 1⁄8 cups
margarine/butter	1 tbs.	1 1⁄4 tbs.	2 tbs.
raisins	1⁄3 cup	1⁄2 cup	2⁄3 cup
sugar	1 tbs.	1 1⁄3 tbs.	2 tbs.
salt	1⁄2 tsp.	2⁄3 tsp.	1 tsp.
bread flour	1 1⁄2 cups	2 cups	3 cups
yeast	1 tsp.	1 1⁄2 tsp.	2 tsp.

Filling

melted margarine	3 tbs.	4 tbs.	6 tbs.
cinnamon	2 tsp.	1 tbs.	1⅓ tbs.
brown sugar	2½ tbs.	3 tbs.	5 tbs.
chopped walnuts	1½ tbs.	2 tbs.	3 tbs.

Mix filling ingredients together. Follow directions for jelly-roll, page 128. Bake in a preheated 350° oven for 30 to 40 minutes or until golden brown and bread makes a hollow sound when tapped.

Glaze

powdered sugar	½ cup (+/-)	¾ cup (+/-)	1 cup (+/-)
milk	1½ tsp.	2 tsp.	3 tsp.
vanilla	⅛ tsp.	⅛ tsp.	¼ tsp.

Mix glaze ingredients until desired consistency — fairly thick. Pour over baked bread while still hot.

PIZZA, MEAT PIES, & HAND PIES

The recipes in this chapter could be served as entrées for lunches, brunches or suppers, accompanied by a tossed salad or a bowl of soup.

If you have a Panasonic SDBT6P or a National SDBT6N you may make some of these on the *Variety Bread Cycle*. This cycle enables you to remove the dough, place fillings into it and replace it into the machine for baking. Follow the directions given in your owner's manual.

Owners of all other machines should make the recipes on the dough setting, remove, fill according to following directions and bake (in your conventional oven). A small amount of flour may be used when rolling dough to prevent it from sticking.

METHODS

JELLY-ROLL - Remove dough from machine and roll into a rectangle. Spread filling (mixed or layered) on top. Starting from the wide end, roll dough jelly-roll fashion to encase filling, pinch ends closed, place on a nonstick baking pan and let rise for about ½ hour.

STROMBOLI - Remove dough from machine and roll into a rectangle. Spread filling ingredients over the middle third of the rectangle so it runs the length of the wide end. Fold one side over top of the filling and then the other side on top of that; pinch ends closed. Place, seam side down, on a lightly buttered baking sheet, cover and let rise for about 30 minutes. Lightly olive oil top, and bake in a preheated 350° oven for 20 to 30 minutes or until done.

CALZONE - Remove dough from machine and roll it into circles of approximately 8 inches. Spread filling on one half of the circle leaving a border around it for closing. Close the calzone by folding the unfilled side on top of the filled side and crimping the edges closed with your fingers or a fork. Place on a lightly greased baking or pizza pan. Let rise approximately 30 minutes.

FOR APPETIZERS - Roll the dough out to a ⅛-inch thickness and cut circles with a glass or biscuit cutter (about 3 inches). Fill and close them the same way as the large calzones but bake in a preheated 450° oven for 25 to 30 minutes.

PIZZA - Remove dough from machine and roll into one or two pizza-pan sized circles. Place on a lightly olive oiled pizza pan and turn any excess dough under itself to form a high crust. Cover and let rise for approximately 30 minutes. Spread toppings on top (either homemade or purchased) — sauce, cheeses, meats, mushrooms, etc., put into a cold oven, turn oven on to 500° and let bake approximately 20 to 30 minutes or until golden brown and cheese is melted. If using the *Three Cheese Sauce* filling for a pizza topping (see page 154), bake in a preheated 400° oven for 25 to 30 minutes.

CALZONE

Choose one of several different fillings for a wonderful meal or make smaller versions for appetizers.

	Small (4)	**Medium (6)**	**Large (8)**
water	⅔ cup	1 cup	1⅓ cups
olive oil	1 tbs.	1½ tbs.	2 tbs.
salt	⅓ tsp.	½ tsp.	⅔ tsp.
oregano	¼ tsp.	⅓ tsp.	½ tsp.
bread flour	2 cups	3 cups	4 cups
yeast	1 tsp.	1½ tsp.	2½ tsp.

Filling

Put 1½ to 2 tbs. each of ricotta and grated mozzarella cheese in each calzone. The strombolli fillings may also be used. Follow directions for calzone, page 141. Brush lightly with olive oil and bake in a preheated 500° oven for approximately 20 to 30 minutes or until puffed and golden.

SAUSAGE BREAD

Terrific hot or cold — serve it sliced at a picnic or tailgate party with red wine.

Dough

	Medium	Large
water	2/3 cup	1 cup
margarine/butter	1 tbs.	1 1/3 tbs.
salt	3/4 tsp.	1 1/4 tsp.
sugar	2/3 tsp.	1 tsp.
bread flour	2 cups	3 cups
yeast	1 1/2 tsp.	2 1/2 tsp.

Filling

	Medium	Large
cooked, chopped sausage	2/3 lb.	1 lb.
grated provolone cheese	2 oz.	3 oz.
grated mozzarella cheese	2 oz.	3 oz.
garlic power	1/8 tsp.	1/4 tsp.
salt and pepper to taste		

Mix filling ingredients together. Follow directions for jelly-roll on page 140. Bake for 30 to 35 minutes in a preheated 350° oven.

MEAT ROLL

My children went wild over this one and want it every night for supper.

Dough

	Medium	Large
water	2/3 cup	1 cup
vegetable oil	2 tsp.	1 tbs.
salt	1/3 tsp.	1/2 tsp.
sugar	2/3 tsp.	1 tsp.
bread flour	1 1/3 cup	2 cups
whole wheat flour	2/3 cup	1 cup
nonfat dry milk	2 tbs.	3 tbs.
yeast	1 tsp.	1 1/2 tsp.

Meat filling

	Medium	Large
cooked sausage	1/3 lb.	1/2 lb.
cooked ground beef or turkey	1/3 lb.	1/2 lb.
Velvetta™ or similar cheese	1/3 lb.	1/2 lb.
salt and pepper to taste		

Cut cheese into 1-inch cubes and mix together with cooked, drained but still hot meats. Cheese should warm enough to serve as the "glue" for the filling. If cheese is not melting into meat, warm in microwave for a minute or two. Follow directions for jelly-roll, page 140, or stromboli on page 141. Bake in a preheated 350° oven for 20 to 25 minutes.

BREAD QUICHE

Bread makes a nice change from pastry, and cuts the richness of this dish a bit.

Dough

	Medium	Large (2)
water	½ cup	⅔ cup
vegetable oil	¾ tsp.	1 tsp.
salt	⅛ tsp.	⅛ tsp.
sugar	¼ tsp.	⅓ tsp.
parsley, optional	⅓ tsp.	½ tsp.
bread flour	1½ cups	2 cups
nonfat dry milk	2 tsp.	1 tbs.
yeast	1 tsp.	1 tsp.

Filling

cooked, crumbled bacon, optional	¼ cup	½ cup
chopped scallions, optional	¼ cup	½ cup
margarine/butter, optional	1 tsp.	2 tsp.
grated Swiss or Gruyére cheese	1 cup	2 cups
eggs, beaten	3	6
cream or milk	½ cup	1 cup
nutmeg, salt and pepper to taste		

Lightly sauté scallions in margarine or butter. In a large bowl, mix together eggs, cream or milk, and season with nutmeg, salt and pepper. Add scallions and/or bacon and grated cheese.

Remove dough from machine and roll into a circle. Place dough into a greased (or sprayed with nonstick spray) 8- or 9-inch pie or round pan and fill with cheese mixture. Bake in a preheated 375° oven for 35 to 40 minutes or until set in the middle.

EMPANADAS

While empanadas are usually made from a pastry dough, you'll love this yeasted version. These can be eaten cold or reheated. Great for picnics.

Dough

	Medium	Large
water	½ cup	1 cup
margarine/butter	1 tbs.	2 tbs.
sugar	½ tsp.	1 tsp.
salt	½ tsp.	1 tsp.
whole wheat flour	¾ cup	1½ cups
bread flour	¾ cup	1½ cups
yeast	1 tsp.	1½ tsp.

Filling

	Medium	Large
ground beef or turkey	½ lb.	1 lb.
chopped onion	½	1
paprika	1 tsp.	2 tsp.
cumin	½ tsp.	1 tsp.
salt	¼ tsp.	½ tsp.

Sauté meat and onions; stir in seasonings, adding a tough of oil if necessary. Follow directions for calzones, page 141. Makes 6 or 12 empanadas. Bake in a preheated 350° oven for 20 to 25 minutes.

STROMBOLI

Thanks to Lt. Morro, USN, for sharing a family recipe on which this is based. Soon to become one of your family favorites too!

Dough

	Medium (1)	Large (2)
water	3/4 cup	1½ cups
margarine/butter	1 tbs.	2 tbs.
salt	½ tsp.	1 tsp.
coarsely ground black pepper	1 tsp.	2 tsp.
sugar	3/4 tsp.	1½ tsp.
bread flour	2 cups	3 cups
yeast	1½ tsp.	2½ tsp.

Fill with one of the fillings that follow, according to instructions on page 141.

Meat Filling

	Medium (1)	Large (2)
grated provolone cheese	¼ to ⅓ cup	½ to ⅔ cup
grated mozzarella cheese	¼ to ⅓ cup	½ to ⅔ cup
diced hard Italian salami	¼ to ⅓ cup	½ to ⅔ cup
diced Italian ham	¼ to ⅓ cup	½ to ⅔ cup

Mix ingredients together.

Spinach Filling

	Medium (1)	Large (2)
1 (10½ oz.) box frozen chopped spinach	1	2
garlic powder	1 tsp.	2 tsp.
olive oil	1 tbs.	2 tbs.
grated provolone cheese	½ cup +/-	1 cup +/-
grated mozzarella cheese	½ cup +/-	1 cup +/-

Sauté thawed spinach in olive oil and garlic powder until all water has evaporated. Mix cheeses into spinach.

Variation: substitute ½ or 1 bag of frozen chopped broccoli for spinach.

Three Cheese Filling or Sauce

This is an excellent topping for pizza or a filling for calzones or stromboli. Don't forget — freshly grated Parmesan is always better than pre-grated Parmesan.

	Small	**Medium**	**Large**
ricotta cheese	1 cup	1½ cups	2 cups
grated Parmesan cheese	½ cup	¾ cup	1 cup
grated mozzarella cheese	½ cup	¾ cup	1 cup
eggs	1	1½	2
parsley	⅔ tsp.	1 tsp.	1⅓ tsp.
basil	⅔ tsp.	1 tsp.	1⅓ tsp.
coarsely ground black pepper	⅓ tsp.	½ tsp.	⅔ tsp.

Mix cheeses and eggs together until well blended. Add seasonings until just mixed in.

PIZZA DOUGH

Pizza will quickly become an often-served meal in your home with this delicious, easy recipe. If you prefer, you can replace the whole wheat flour with bread flour.

	1 Small	1 Large	2 Small
water	⅔ cup	1 cup	1⅓ cups
olive oil	2 tsp.	1 tbs.	1⅓ tbs.
salt	⅓ tsp.	½ tsp.	⅔ tsp.
oregano, optional	1 tsp.	1½ tsp.	2 tsp.
whole wheat flour	1 cup	1½ cups	2 cups
bread flour	1 cup	1½ cups	2 cups
yeast	1 tsp.	1½ tsp.	2½ tsp.

Follow directions for pizza, page 142.

Note: This may also be made using any pizza topping and following directions for jelly-roll, page 140. Brush lightly with a little olive oil and bake in a preheated 400° oven for about 30 minutes.

FOCACCIA

Say foh-CAH-chee-ah. This cousin to pizza, cut into small wedges or squares, is the perfect accompaniment to soups or salads. Or serve as an appetizer or with a buffet. Delicious served hot or cold, as a snack or with a meal.

	1 Large	**2 Small**	**2 Large**
water	½ cup	⅔ cup	1 cup
olive oil	1½ tbs.	2 tbs.	3 tbs.
vegetable oil	¼ cup	⅓ cup	½ cup
salt	¼ tsp.	⅓ tsp.	½ tsp.
basil or rosemary	⅔ tsp.	1 tsp.	1⅓ tsp.
sugar	1½ tsp.	2 tsp.	1 tbs.
bread flour	2¼ cups	3 cups	4½ cups
yeast	1 tsp.	1½ tsp.	2 tsp.

Remove dough from machine and, using your fingers, press the dough onto a lightly greased pizza pan or baking sheet. Cover and let rise for about 30 minutes. Spread topping over dough and bake in a preheated 375° oven for about 30 minutes.

Topping

garlic powder	⅛ tsp.	⅛ tsp.	¼ tsp.
olive oil	2 tbs.	3 tbs.	¼ cup
basil or rosemary	2 tsp.	1 tbs.	1⅓ tbs.
sea salt, optional	1 tsp.	1½ tsp.	2 tsp.

Mix ingredients together.

RUEBEN ROLL

This is a quick and easy way to make several Ruebens — great for picnics or tailgating parties. Substitute mustard for Thousand Island dressing if preferred.

Dough

	1 Medium	1 Large	2 Medium
water	⅔ cup	1 cup	1⅓ cups
vegetable oil	2 tsp.	1 tbs.	1⅓ tbs.
salt	¼ tsp.	⅓ tsp.	½ tsp.
sugar	¼ tsp.	⅓ tsp.	½ tsp.
unsweetened cocoa	1 tbs.	1½ tbs.	2 tbs.
caraway seeds	1 tsp.	1½ tsp.	2 tsp.
rye flour	⅔ cup	1 cup	1⅓ cups
bread flour	1⅓ cup	2 cups	2⅔ cups
yeast	1 tsp.	1½ tsp.	2 tsp.

Filling

Layer in order given:

Thousand Island dressing	2 tbs.	3 tbs.	¼ tbs.
drained sauerkraut	⅓ cup	½ cup	⅔ cup
grated Swiss cheese	⅓ cup	½ cup	⅔ cup
corned beef, cubed	½ cup	¾ cup	1 cup

Follow directions for either jelly-roll, page 140, or strombolli, page 141. Bake in a preheated 350° oven for 25 to 30 minutes.

MINI CHEESE BREADS

This recipe is based on a recipe for a Turkish cheese bread. These make great appetizers, lunch or a light dinner with a salad. (I even pack these for school/work lunches for a nice change of pace.) Serve either hot or cold.

	Small(5)	Medium(8)	Large(10)
cream cheese	4 oz.	6 oz.	8 oz.
ricotta cheese	¾ cup	1⅛ cups	1½ cups
grated Parmesan cheese	½ cup	⅔ cup	1 cup
parsley	1 tbs.	1½ tbs.	2 tbs.
dried chives	2 tsp.	1 tbs.	1⅓ tbs.

Mix ingredients together. Use pizza or calzone dough, omitting the oregano. Divide dough into 5, 8 or 10 balls and roll into circles or small rectangles; fold edges up so that you have a small crust. Divide the cheese filling between the dough pieces and fill each one. Place on a greased baking sheet, let rise 20 minutes, and bake in a preheated 375° oven for 25 minutes or until golden brown.

CAKES & QUICK BREADS

WARNING! Cakes and quick breads (non-yeast breads) may, at this time, only be made in the Zojirushi, National SD-BT6N or Panasonic SD-T6P machines. Do not attempt making these in any other machines as the results will fail.

The recipes in this chapter use self-rising flour. If substituting all-purpose flour, add 1½ tsp. of baking powder and ½ tsp. of salt for each cup of flour used.

If you are using a National or Panasonic machine, all ingredients are mixed together prior to placing in the pan for baking. Any ingredients listed following asterisks are to be mixed in last and only until blended. As you must tell the machine how long to bake the quick breads/cakes, the times are given in each recipe.

If using the Zojirushi, place the ingredients in the machine in the order given. Any ingredients listed following asterisks are to be added at the "beep." As the machine is preprogrammed to turn off when the cakes/quick breads are completely baked, you may ignore the baking times.

Consult your owner's manual for directions on how to use the different cake/quick bread cycles.

PUMPKIN OATMEAL BREAD

Autumn cannot pass by without this bread in the house. Fresh pumpkin really makes a difference if you have the time to prepare it. If desired, frost with a cream cheese frosting and serve as a delicious cake.

1/3 cup vegetable oil
1 cup fresh pumpkin puree (or 8 oz.
  canned pumpkin)
2 eggs
3/4 cup brown sugar, packed
1/8 tsp. nutmeg

1/4 tsp. cloves
1 1/2 tsp. cinnamon
3/4 cup oats
1 1/4 cups self-rising flour
***
1/4 cup ground walnuts

Bake for 40 minutes.

To prepare fresh pumpkin puree, simply cut pumpkin in half, removing stem, pulp and seeds. Cut pumpkin into four to five inch squares and place in boiling water until soft and fork pierces easily. Drain off water and puree pumpkin in food processor or blender. Pumpkin is easily placed in ziplock bags, premeasured into one or two cups, and kept frozen until required for baking.

SPOON BREAD

A "southern" must, truly delicious.

1 cup sour cream (8 oz.)
1 (8¾ oz.) can corn, drained
1 (8¾ oz.) can creamed corn
½ cup margarine/butter, softened

2 eggs
¾ cup cornmeal
¾ cup self-rising flour

Bake for 60 minutes.

STRAWBERRY OR PEACH BREAD

A wonderful bread for holiday entertaining.

⅓ cup milk
⅔ cup strawberry, peach or other
  preserves
3 eggs
½ tsp. vanilla extract
½ cup butter/margarine softened

½ cup sugar
⅔ cup oats
1⅓ cups self-rising flour
***
⅓ cup ground walnuts or pecans,
  optional

Bake for 60 minutes.

164 CAKES & QUICK BREADS

APPLE CAKE

Delicious served hot with or without vanilla ice cream.

2 cups diced apples
1 egg
¼ cup vegetable oil
¼ tsp. cinnamon
½ tsp. baking soda

¾ cup sugar
1 cup self-rising flour
***

¼ cup ground walnuts or pecans

An electric beater or mixer should be used for this as the apples must be very well blended, providing moisture to the batter. Bake for 50 minutes.

CARROT CAKE

Well worth the few moments to grind up the carrots. May be frosted with a cream cheese frosting if desired. Or simply eaten with cream cheese.

1 cup grated carrots
½ cup + 2 tbs. vegetable oil
2 eggs
1 cup sugar
1 tsp. cinnamon

¾ tsp. baking soda
½ cup oats
1 cup self-rising flour
***

¼ cup ground walnuts or pecans

Bake for 45 minutes.

CHOCOLATE CHOCOLATE CHIP CAKE

If you like chocolate, you'll make this one over and over and over! You can substitute mint chocolate chips or peanut butter chips.

1/4 cup vegetable oil
1/2 tsp. vanilla extract
1/2 cup milk
2 eggs

1 1/2 cups Devils Food cake mix with pudding (approx. 1/2 box)
***
1/2-3/4 cup chocolate chips

Bake for 35 minutes.

POPPY SEED CAKE

A wonderful cake for holidays or any time of the year. One of the all-time favorites at my house.

3/4 cup milk
2 eggs
1/2 cup vegetable oil
1 tsp. butter flavoring
1 tsp. almond extract

1 tsp. vanilla extract
1 tbs. poppy seeds
1 cup sugar
1 1/2 cups self-rising flour

Bake for 50 minutes.

SOURCES

Arrowhead Mills, Inc. (806) 364-0730
Box 866
Hereford, TX 79045

A wide variety of grains and flours. Mail order and health food store supplier.

Balducci's (800) 822-1444
9th Street & 6th Ave.
New York, NY 10011

Italian foods, mozzarella cheese. Candied fruits. Mail order.

Dean & Deluca (800) 221-7714
560 Broadway
New York, NY 10012

Mail order - specialty and gourmet foods.

Ener-G Foods (800) 331-5222
P. O. Box 84487
Seattle, WA 98124-5787

Gluten free bread mixes for bread machines. Egg replacer powder. Mail order.

Garden Spot Distributors (800) 829-5100
438 White Oak Road
New Holland, PA 17557

Mail order of a wide variety of whole grains, flours, cereals, etc.

Great Valley Mills (215) 256-6648
687 Mill Road
Telford, PA 18969

Mail order of stone ground flours, etc.

King Arthur Flour (802) 649-3881
RRT #2 Box 56
Norwich, VT 05055

Mail order catalog of flours, grains and other items.

Morgan's Mills   (207) 785-4900
RD2 Box 4602
Union, ME 04862

Mail order - stone ground flours, natural and gourmet foods.

The Vermont Country Store
(802) 362-4647
P.O. Box 3000
Manchester Center, VT 05255-3000

Mail order - stone ground flours and cereals and other items.

Walnut Acres (800) 433-3998
Penns Creek, PA 17862

Mail order organic farm. Flours, grains, etc.

INDEX

SERVE CREATIVE, EASY, NUTRITIOUS MEALS WITH NITTY GRITTY® COOKBOOKS

The Bread Machine Cookbook
The Bread Machine Cookbook II
The Sandwich Maker Cookbook
The Juicer Book
Bread Baking (traditional), revised
The Kid's Cookbook, revised
The Kid's Microwave Cookbook
15-Minute Meals for 1 or 2
Recipes for the 9x13 Pan
Turkey, the Magic Ingredient
Chocolate Cherry Tortes and Other Lowfat Delights
Lowfat American Favorites
Lowfat International Cuisine
The Hunk Cookbook
Now That's Italian!
Fabulous Fiber Cookery

Low Salt, Low Sugar, Low Fat Desserts
What's for Breakfast?
Healthy Cooking on the Run
Healthy Snacks for Kids
Creative Soups & Salads
Quick & Easy Pasta Recipes
Muffins, Nut Breads and More
The Barbecue Book
The Wok
New Ways with Your Wok
Quiche & Soufflé Cookbook
Easy Microwave Cooking
Compleat American House- wife 1787
Cooking for 1 or 2
Brunch
Cocktails & Hors d'Oeuvres

Meals in Minutes
New Ways to Enjoy Chicken
Favorite Seafood Recipes
No Salt, No Sugar, No Fat Cookbook
The Fresh Vegetable Cookbook
Modern Ice Cream Recipes
Crepes & Omelets
Time-Saving Gourmet Cooking
New International Fondue Cookbook
Extra-Special Crockery Pot Recipes
Favorite Cookie Recipes
Authentic Mexican Cooking
Fisherman's Wharf Cookbook
The Best of Nitty Gritty
The Creative Lunch Box

Write or call for our free catalog.
Bristol Publishing Enterprises, Inc.
P.O. Box 1737, San Leandro, CA 94577
(800)346-4889; in California (510)895-4461